The Facts of Food

ARNOLD E. BENDER

The Facts of Food

OXFORD UNIVERSITY PRESS
LONDON   OXFORD   NEW YORK
1975

Oxford University Press, Ely House, London W.1

GLASGOW NEW YORK TORONTO MELBOURNE WELLINGTON
CAPE TOWN IBADAN NAIROBI DAR ES SALAAM LUSAKA ADDIS ABABA
DELHI BOMBAY CALCUTTA MADRAS KARACHI LAHORE DACCA
KUALA LUMPUR SINGAPORE HONG KONG TOKYO

PAPERBACK ISBN 0 19 289046 8
CASEBOUND ISBN 0 19 217632 3

© OXFORD UNIVERSITY PRESS 1975

First published in the Oxford Paperbacks University Series 1975
and simultaneously in a cloth bound edition

Printed in Great Britain by
Northumberland Press Limited, Gateshead

Contents

I

Taken three times a day

It is possible to live, even in Europe, on about 6p a day, yet we each spend about 6op. The 6p buys enough to keep body and soul together, that is, to supply the nutrients that we need to maintain health; the rest of the money buys the taste, variety, textures, colours, and convenience. It is the difference between getting the vitamin C we need from soggy cabbage or fresh strawberries, or our protein from cowpeas or caviare.

What we need to keep body and soul bound together firmly enough to keep in good health, where we can get it, how much we need, why we like the flavours and colours, and why we select caviare (sometimes) instead of cowpeas comprise the study of nutrition.

WHAT IS NUTRITION?

A whole book would be needed to define nutrition completely, but a shorter definition is possible. 'The science of nutrition' may be defined as the study of food in relation to man, and the study of man in relation to his food. Both halves of this definition have equal weight.

This sounds like a very broad field of study and, indeed, it is. Its breadth is illustrated by the diagram (Fig. 1.1), which shows how nutrition stretches from soil to cell, including a great part of man's activities on the way.

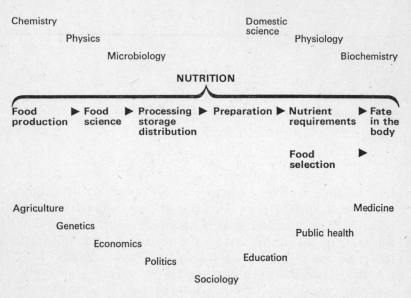

FIG. 1.1. The science of nutrition covers a wide range of disciplines.

Food production

The study of food starts with its production. The nutrition-ist is not a food producer, but he has direct interests in food production. Indeed, today his interest starts even before the food is produced, since in recent years he has been closely involved with the geneticist and the farmer in pro-ducing new strains of both plants and animals which yield more and better food.

Before the animal geneticist can produce better strains of animals that are more resistant to disease and faster growing with greater feed-conversion efficiency, and before the farmer can produce the highest yields of milk or meat or eggs for the least cost, the animal nutritionist has to formulate diets—the optimum supply of energy, protein, vitamins, and minerals—that give maximum growth of livestock.

This problem is complicated by finding, for example, that a chicken does not need the same food for maximum growth as for maximum egg production, and that the needs of the adult animal are not the same as those of its young. Feeding cattle for their milk or for their meat, or feeding their offspring all call for different amounts of nutrients in different proportions to give the highest efficiency.

The nutritionist is also involved in the production of food from rather unusual sources. Food production today is not limited to the farmer, nor is it necessarily dependent on soil; the chemical engineer and the laboratory technician are already producing foods—or at least basic foodstuffs from which foods can be made—in tanks and factories, from such unlikely raw materials as petroleum residues, sawdust, sewage, and wool. A variety of foods can be produced by texturing vegetable protein to make it look like meat or fish or fruit, by synthesis from chemical raw materials, by growing bacteria, moulds, yeast, and algae, or by converting animal feed into human food.

These are, in many instances, not new ideas, but until now there has been little need to develop them. Some, in fact, were suggested hundreds of years ago; they are novel rather than new. The nutritionist is involved because the bacteria, moulds, yeasts, and algae have their own nutritional needs which must be determined and satisfied before they can be grown efficiently, and we also need to know the nutritional value of these unusual foods when they are fed to man or his animals.

Food storage and distribution

After the food has been produced, whether from plants, animals, or factory, it has to be stored, distributed over great distances, and often stored again. This may sound a simple, efficient operation, but it is not. Much food is lost in the field, or destroyed by pests and microbes; and a great deal more is lost in store, by chemical and enzymic deterioration or by attack from vermin, birds, insects, moulds,

and all the other living creatures who need food just as much
as man does.

Distribution on a large scale is a modern development:
refrigerated ships, gas storage, and fast transport are all
recent inventions. The length of time that food will keep
wholesome during transport, in the warehouse, in the shops,
and in the domestic larder, depends a great deal on the
skill of the food technologist. Cellophane wrapping, plastic
laminates, foil pouches—the variety of packaging that pro-
longs shelf-life—are all new. Preservation by drying, heating, and smoking has been carried out for centuries; quick-
freezing, irradiation, and canning are developments of
modern science and technology.

Before the modern development of food technology, say
the last century, there was a much smaller variety of foods
available, shelf-life was shorter, most foods were locally
grown, and much less was transported across the world.
Processing was in its infancy and there were relatively few
manufactured foods. Before the development of canning
and refrigeration in the nineteenth century, people ate
well immediately after the harvest but not so well between
harvests.

In many parts of the world this is still the position today.
It is only in the industrialized communities that the seasons
are ignored and food is abundant all the year round. In
the less developed communities people still wait anxiously
for the next harvest, and have very few processed foods.

The role of the nutritionist in this field is to help to
maintain the nutrients that might deteriorate during processing, transport, and storage; to help to select raw materials of high nutritive value; and to add nutrients when
necessary.

Nutritional requirements

In his own area of specialization the nutritionist bears the
responsibility of determining the amounts and proportions
of the various nutrients that are needed by man, his wife,
and children, both in health and disease, at work and rest,

during recovery from illness, in pregnancy and lactation, and in old age. Chemistry, physiology, and biochemistry are his main tools.

Much information has been revealed through studying disease patterns of communities throughout the world. Some diseases are commoner in certain areas where particular foods are in short supply—this is one of the approaches that led to the discovery of the vitamins. The fate of foods in the body can often be revealed by studying people in whom the normal pattern of metabolism has become deranged.

Thus the nutritionist can provide the required information—within limits. The cook has then to produce the foods in an acceptable form.

Eating habits

Despite the best of advice people often do not eat the right foods, even when they are available. In equatorial regions children, in particular, suffer blindness as a result of insufficient vitamin A, although the pawpaw and red palm oil, both rich sources of this vitamin, are readily available. In parts of Africa there are lake and riverside dwellers whose children suffer protein deficiency while the remedy —fish—is abundant on their doorsteps. There is scurvy while the cure hangs on the trees.

A host of factors control what people eat. Obviously the starting point is whether or not the food is available, and this may depend on climate and soil. Price is obviously important, but so also are traditions, culture, social background, prejudices, and customs. Why is it that most of us in the West will buy cabbage or endive from the greengrocer while we discard the dandelions that grow freely on the lawn? Some people certainly eat dandelion leaves; why not everyone? Some tribes in Africa eat the leaves of particular plants while their neighbours, who live in the same village but originate from another tribe, do not.

When the nutritionist tries to find out why people eat what they do, or to change their eating habits—an extremely difficult operation—he wanders into the realms of sociology and psychology. When mother made us clear all the food from our plates did she implant the habit of eating everything, or make us hate those foods forever? Certainly the television advertiser has more influence over our eating habits than the nutritionist, and many people tend to follow the habits of the temporary idol, whether football hero or pop star, rather than accept scientific advice.

Biochemistry

Finally, the study of nutrition finishes with the fate of the foods in the body. This provides a guide to what and how much we need, and why, as well as information about the interactions between nutrients and other factors in the environment, such as drugs, pollution, and stress.

So 'nutrition' involves the basic sciences of chemistry, physics, physiology, and biochemistry, as well as a range of the applied sciences, and it enters fields such as genetics, politics, sociology, education, psychology, and the law. The all-embracing definition of the science of nutrition—as the study of man in relation to his food as well as the study of food in relation to man—is not too broad. Social and political changes have affected man's eating habits, but so also have man's eating habits caused widespread social and political changes.

FOOD AND MANKIND

Since food is one of the three essentials of life, it is not surprising that it has been, and is, the centre of great social and political change. In fact, of the three essentials of life— food, shelter and clothing—the second and third can be dispensed with (under appropriate climatic circumstances), so that the empty stomach becomes the great motivator of the human race. Esau sold his birthright for bread and a potage of lentils; it was famine in the Middle East that brought Jacob and his family to settle in Egypt; and it was famine in Ireland 4000 years later that established more

Irish in the United States than in Ireland. We are told that Napoleon lost the battle of Leipzig by making serious tactical errors because he was sluggish after a heavy meal (of shoulder of mutton stuffed with onions), and that the retreat from Caporetto in the First World War—a blot on the honour of the Italian army—was due to the low calorie allowance of the Italian troops. The Indian mutiny was triggered off by the use of pig fat on the cartridges. It was the search for spices, which were food preservatives before the days of modern food technology, that stimulated the exploration leading to the colonization of India. Scurvy defeated some of the earlier explorations. It is also reported that only the strong advice of Benjamin Franklin persuaded the British to take Canada after the war with the French, rather than the very attractive sugar-rich island of Guadeloupe.

It is not always realized by city folk how great a part of man's activities is devoted solely to the production of food. Two-thirds of the people in the world devote their lives to feeding themselves and the other one-third. Hence all the so-called achievements of mankind, from radio to moon rocketry, the creative arts, the manufacture of shelter and transport, and the multitude of factors that contribute to our daily comfort, are the work of only one-third of the human race—the other two-thirds do little but produce food.

The mechanization of farming, which has allowed a few countries to devote most of their time to the arts, the sciences, and the production of luxuries, is of recent and rapid growth. In the United States—one of the world's largest producers of both food and trivia—150 years ago (1820), 25 per cent of the population were farmers, so one farm-worker fed 4 people; at the beginning of this century (1900) things had improved a little and he fed 7 people; 50 years later this number had risen to 16; but between 1950 and 1969 the number increased threefold to 47. This was due to the combined efforts of plant and animal geneticists and plant and animal nutritionists and to the use of irrigation, fertilizers, and pesticides, but mainly to the mechanization of farming. But we are now informed that mechanization in some farms in the United States has reached such a stage that farming, a process intended to trap the free energy of the sunshine for the benefit of man, can cost as much in energy input in the form of fertilizers, chemicals, and tractor fuel as is obtained in the form of calories from the food produced. On this basis the peasant farmers of Nepal, comprising 92 per cent of the population there and having no aid other than the water buffalo, are far more efficient than the soil technocrats of America.

ACTIONS AND INTERACTIONS: THE STORY OF MARGARINE

Of the many examples that could be selected to illustrate the interactions between food and the social scene, margarine is a good choice, since it has already celebrated its hundredth birthday (in 1969). Margarine was invented as a cheap substitute for butter, and until very recently—and in some areas still—served as a social distinction between mistress and servant. Although margarine was invented in France, Holland became the centre of manufacture in the early days, because the Dutch found it so profitable to export their butter to Great Britain. Thirty years later, during the First World War, another butter-producer, Denmark, exported most of her butter to Great Britain and so deprived many of her people of their source of vitamin A. As a result there was widespread xerophthalmia, the vitamin A deficiency disease. This, in turn, led to the practice of adding synthetic vitamins to foods when there is a demonstrable shortage.

Chemistry, as always in food technology, played a vital role in the development of margarine. First, refining procedures allowed the use of a variety of fats in place of the original beef tallow, and secondly, the principles of hydrogenation, which allowed the use of any oil, were developed by Sabatier and Senderens in 1901. One of these sources was whale oil, the demand for which has brought about one of our current ecological problems.

The development of the techniques of chemical analysis

has played a part in recent progress. For example, gas chromatography, a technique which is used to detect small amounts of volatile substances (for example, in the breath-test for alcohol) has helped in the identification of the flavouring compounds in butter (always the flavour model for margarine). This culminated in 1964 with the discovery of the chemical responsible for butter's typical creamy flavour. The chemical, known as *cis*-4-heptanal, is so potent that its flavour can be detected when only a few milligrams are added to a tonne of margarine—a concentration of a few parts per thousand million.

While we might well expect our foods to be altered by technical achievements and by social change, what might have been less expected was the profound effect that the demand for foodstuffs had on the social conditions in a large part of the world (as has been described by Dr. Magnus Pyke).

For example, in West Africa the land was owned in the past by the community, and according to local custom the crops, such as palm nuts, were either the perquisites of the woman or man who planted the tree, or they belonged to the community. The entire social system was changed by the incursion of the Western business men, who set up large-scale plantations to provide fats for the manufacture of margarine. Technology, machinery, the utilization of by-products, and the introduction of money values changed the lives of these communities; similar changes took place in Indonesia, Oceania, Nigeria, and the Belgian Congo.

Even politics have been involved in margarine product-ion, oddly enough in an interaction with psychology. Dairy interests have, from time to time, reacted strongly against any competitor, and one line of defence against margarine was to ban (by law) the addition of the yellow colour which makes margarine look like butter. The effect of being offered a fat-spread that is white in place of the usual colour —an interesting point in the psychology of food selection— is as off-putting as yellow tomatoes, white chocolate, or the black-iced wedding cake once shown at the London Baking Exhibition, and sales of margarine were consequently low.

The latest factor in the marketing of margarine is again nutritional. This is the suggestion that polyunsaturated fats, which can be incorporated into margarine in high concentration, lower the level of blood cholesterol and so may help to prevent heart disease. In some quarters this factor has already overcome the social barriers to the consumption of margarine, and recently it brought about a change in legislation. Strict laws protect the butter industry in New Zealand by prohibiting the import of margarine. On behalf of people suffering from heart disease, a New Zealand M.P. campaigned for the import of polyunsaturated margarine. This was finally permitted, and patients may now obtain this margarine—but only with a doctor's certificate, and even then they may not consume more than N.Z. $20 worth per year.

THE SOCIAL INFLUENCE OF SUGAR

Sugar has been the centre of great changes in society. It was the direct cause of the slave trade—starting at the end of the fifteenth century, when slaves were transported to sugar plantations, and continuing for the next 300 years. Great advances in technology have made a product that was an expensive luxury for 4000 years into a cheap food for everyone. People in Great Britain ate about 2 kg of sugar per head in 1850 and now eat 20 times as much. It accounts for about one-fifth of the total food intake in terms of energy. We suffer diseases today that existed rarely, if at all, a hundred years ago, and this raises the question of whether sugar is a cause of the diseases.

FROM PREHISTORIC TO MODERN FOOD

Man has been on earth for several millions of years, and for the whole of that time he has eaten food. Since he is still here the food must have been adequate, although some groups of people may have died out, and many may have survived in a rather poor state.

Man is called omnivorous—he eats everything: chips, snails, witchedy grubs, seaweed, beans on toast, and even tomato ketchup. His ancestors seem to have started out largely as vegetarians, eating the roots and shoots of wild plants, and their nuts, fruits, and bulbs, probably with a few insects, eggs, perhaps grubs, and small animals that they could easily catch without much in the way of weaponry. Indeed, this is still the food of some primitive tribes today.

Then, about 15 million years ago, we are told that drought caused the forests to retreat, and man's ancestors came down from the trees to stand on their own feet. So about 5 or 6 million years ago he became more of a seed-eater. It is suggested that he did not at that time have the weapons to kill large animals, and so did not compete with carnivores, but lived in harmony with them.

Man developed tools about 3 million years ago, and added meat to his larder. A great change came about when he learned how to use fire, about 400 000 years ago. Cooking, the first food process to be invented, breaks down the hard, fibrous tissues and makes them digestible, so the range of the diet could be greatly extended. Fire meant a hearth and probably a semi-permanent settlement to serve as a basis for hunting.

It is only in recent times, say about 10 000 years ago, that man decided to cultivate crops instead of gathering food from the countryside, and that he settled down and built towns. This caused probably the greatest change in his diet in the millions of years of his development, because cereal crops are largely starch, and so it is likely that man considerably increased the proportion of starch in his diet. Whether we have yet adapted to this change—10 000 years is a short time in the development of a species—we do not know.

Modern food processing started early in the nineteenth century. New types of food were added to the menu. Sugar became an increasing part of the diet. Pre-cooked, low-fibre, pre-gelatinized, processed, enriched, canned, sterilized, irradiated, and frozen foods became our daily fare. Are

they the cause of man's better health (as measured by longer
expectancy of life, lower infant mortality, and eradication
of many diseases) or his worse health (as measured by the
increased incidence of cancer, heart disease, diverticular
disease, and all the maladies of affluence)? To be honest,
we do not know.

NUTRITION AS A SCIENCE

The science of nutrition has passed through two main
stages. The first stage led to the discovery of the nutrients
and man's need for them: the 20 vitamins, the 20 amino
acids in proteins, the 20 or 30 mineral salts, and the need
for energy. When nutrients were not plentifully supplied
children grew more slowly, and when they were added to
the diet growth rates speeded up. Table 1.1 shows the experiment that led to the provision of school milk. The
addition of certain foods increased the height and weight

TABLE 1.1

*The experiment that started the provision
of school milk*

Diet	Increase after 1 year	
	Weight (pounds)†	Height (inches)‡
Basic diet	3·85	1·84
plus 1 pint milk	6·98	2·63
or same energy as sugar	4·93	1·94
or same energy as butter	6·30	2·22
or water cress	5·42	1·70
or milk casein	5·21	1·84
or margarine (unenriched)	4·01	1·76

Experiments of Dr. C. Mann (1922).

Growth improved by foods with vitamin A (milk, butter, watercress) and
protein (milk, milk casein).

† 1 lb=0·45 kg.
‡ 1 in=25·4 mm.

of children, because they had been short of nutrients supplied in the added foods.

Thus it became possible to compile an adequate diet and to cure and prevent the various deficiency diseases common in many countries. This phase of discovery may not yet be over—it was as recently as 1955 that chromium was shown to restore the impaired metabolism of glucose in some elderly patients; in 1961 zinc was first shown to be a dietary essential; and, although vitamin E has been known for 40 years, it was only in 1962 that it was shown to be essential for human beings.

The second stage in the development of nutrition is more complex. As the older infectious diseases have been largely wiped out by advances in medical science, new diseases have taken their place. Since these are common not only to all industrialized countries but even to the industrialized cities of developing countries, they have been called diseases of affluence. They include heart disease, disorders of the bowel, diabetes, varicose veins, and many others. Nutrition is somehow involved, but only as one of many causes. During the time that these diseases have become common almost all things around us have changed as well as our food. We may well be eating more fat and sugar, more preserved foods, and less bread than earlier generations, but we also breathe in more petrol fumes, pay more for taxes, and watch television. So it is very difficult to find out whether or not foods are involved, and, if so, which ones.

At the same time the study of nutrition has become more complex as new discoveries are made. We now need to consider not only the amount of fat that we eat, but also the different types of fat; not only the carbohydrate, but also what form it is in. We can no longer think of proteins, minerals, and vitamins individually, but must pay attention to their interrelationships. The nutrients appear to be as closely related as the springs on a mattress—tread on one and the others move.

Successes in the treatment of disease through diet are numerous. Various heart and kidney conditions are treated with low-sodium diets, some liver disorders by high-protein diets. There are high- and low-fibre diets, diets low in cholesterol, and a host of others. This is the field of the hospital dietitian. What is more interesting, perhaps, is the relatively recent discovery that some people are born with diseases that can be treated only by dietary modifications. These are the so-called genetic diseases, or inborn errors of metabolism (to be discussed later), they are all of recent discovery, and one naturally wonders how many more such diseases may be common in the community and susceptible to dietary control. We also wonder how much disease is caused by an individual's intolerance to certain foods, wrong selections, alterations in processing, or by natural toxins.

MYTHS AND FACTS

Myths abound in every aspect of life, and food myths are many. Some old wives' tales gain respectability with age, and some appear to be verified when new knowledge comes to light. For example, there was an old wives' tale which taught the value of mouldy buns in the treatment of various infections; the discovery of penicillin in moulds 'proved' how true this was, and how foolish the scientists had been to pooh-pooh these gems of ancient wisdom! (In fact, however, the mouldy buns most likely contained the wrong kind of mould, since very few types have any therapeutic effect; and the dose that a mouldy bun could provide, even were it the right type of mould, would be far too small to have any effect.)

Similarly, when nutritionists learn that various combinations of food, such as cereals and legumes, complement one another by balancing their proteins, they find that housewives across the world have done this for centuries by mixing dishes of rice and peas or maize and beans, not to balance amino acids, but simply because people liked the taste of such mixtures.

Sometimes it is possible to trace the origin of the tales. It is generally accepted that spinach is 'good for you', and many a child has suffered for this reason. In fact, spinach is no better than most other green leafy foods, providing a small amount of vitamins A and C, some iron, and only traces of other nutrients. The belief is largely fostered by the Hollywood films based on the muscular development of Popeye the Sailorman, who rapidly gained in strength after eating canned (why not fresh?) spinach. But the belief pre-dates Hollywood, and appears to be due to an experimental or printing error. Food analyses published in 1870 showed spinach to be exceptionally rich in iron. Anaemia caused by iron deficiency was common, so people were urged to eat spinach. The figure of the high iron content of spinach was regularly reprinted in text books until 1937, when spinach was re-analysed and found to contain only one-tenth of the value originally reported—the fame of spinach may well have grown from a misplaced decimal point.

It is not quite so clear why bread crusts are supposed to make hair curly or why fish is said to be good for the brain, but these sayings are equally untrue. Nor have esoteric foods such as buckwheat, sesame seed, honey, and yogurt any particular virtues—they are very ordinary foods in many parts of the world. The witchedy grub is certainly an unusual food to the Englishman but not to the Australian aborigine; black pudding and tripe may be unusual in London but certainly not in Liverpool.

2

What do we need?

Probably the most important question that the nutritionist has to answer is, What do we need to keep us in good health, and how much? The 'What?' is easier to answer than the 'How much?' and that is what we shall consider here.

Wherever man lives and whatever types of foods he eats, he needs proteins and mineral salts for the construction of body tissues, fats and carbohydrates for energy, and vitamins and other mineral salts to assist in the carrying out of body functions. These substances are called nutrients. They are all obtained from foods and very many foods can supply them—fish and chips, maize and beans, rice and snails. *What* man needs has come to light only in the last hundred years, partly from observation of food habits as related to health and disease, and partly from direct experimentation.

It is more difficult to be precise about how much of each nutrient is needed, largely because of the enormous variation between individuals. Even two people of the same age, height, weight, and sex, doing the same work, may need different amounts. This is simply what the biologist calls biological variation. It seems that, just as our faces differ from one another, our metabolism and dietary needs may also differ—not in kind but in amount. On top of this, human beings appear to adapt well to temporary shortages and surpluses without any obvious change. This makes it difficult to measure the precise amounts of nutrients needed.

HISTORICAL EVIDENCE

Some nutritional disorders and their cures have been known for centuries. Some 3500 years ago an Egyptian medical treatise recommended that people unable to see properly at night should eat roast ox liver or the liver of a black cock. The inability to see in dim light is night-blindness, the earliest sign of a vitamin A deficiency; and we now know that liver is curative because it contains vitamin A.

Scurvy, the result of a shortage of vitamin C, was observed hundreds of years ago among sailors. Vitamin C is obtained from fruits and vegetables, which were not available on long voyages in the days before canning and refrigeration. Rickets, caused by vitamin D deficiency, was known as the English disease. The title was a little unfair, since the disease was common in Northern Europe as a whole, being due to the relative lack of sunshine in that area. Vitamin D can be obtained from food but it is unique in that it can be made in the skin under the influence of sunshine.

A great deal of knowledge about the working of the body and the cure of disease accumulated over the centuries, but there was no systematic understanding of the role of food. Despite this lack of knowledge, farmers managed to feed their animals and mothers managed to feed their babies. However, they did not always feed them very well, and we now know that both animals and babies are healthier, grow faster, and live longer when they receive their full quota of nutrients. Systematic discoveries in the science of nutrition had to wait upon developments in chemistry and physiology late in the nineteenth century, and the fuller understanding of the role of the nutrients in the body came after the more recent developments in the science of biochemistry.

BERI-BERI

The history of beri-beri, a disease now known to be caused by a shortage of vitamin B1, is a good example of how nutritional discoveries were made. Beri-beri was recognized

in China as early as 2600 B.C. and is thought to be the
earliest documented deficiency disease. Victims suffer weak-
ness of the legs and wastage of the muscles (although this
can be masked by oedema—swollen tissues), there is damage
to the heart and the nerves and, when the shortage of the
vitamin is severe and prolonged, the disease is fatal.

The first indication that it was connected with diet came
from observations in the Japanese Navy in 1880. The
Director-General, Takaki, observed that between 1878 and
1883 the British Navy was fairly healthy, whereas about
one-third of all Japanese sailors fell ill every year with
beri-beri. The Japanese diet was mostly rice with fish and
some vegetables, and Takaki believed that this poor diet
caused beri-beri. He added meat, vegetables, barley, and
condensed milk to the sailors' meals, and the men were
cured. Takaki concluded that this was because of the extra
protein.

The true explanation did not come to light until the work
of Drs Eijkman and Grijns between 1896 and 1901. Eijkman was a military doctor in the Dutch East Indies, and
he used chickens for his medical research. To save on the
cost of food, he fed them scraps from the ward of the
military hospital, mainly cooked polished rice (that is, rice
from which the outer brown husk and the germ have been
rubbed off). The chickens developed an unexpected and
obscure paralysis somewhat similar to human beri-beri.
The explanation came when a newly appointed director
of the hospital refused to let Dr. Eijkman have the food
scraps. He was forced to feed the chickens on whole brown
rice (which we now know is rich in vitamin B1), and the
birds recovered.

In 1896 it was difficult for scientists to accept the idea
that disease might be caused by something being absent
from the diet. Not long before, Pasteur had finally persuaded
the scientific world that micro-organisms could cause disease,
so it was natural at that time to assume that all diseases were
caused in this way. It was Grijns in 1901 who correctly
interpreted Eijkman's findings.

The beri-beri story took a long time to complete. It was

another 20 years before a chemically pure substance, thiamin
or vitamin B1, was isolated from the rice bran, and it was
not chemically identified and synthesized until 1937. Meanwhile, in the late 1920s, even before the substance had been
chemically identified, its biochemical effects were being
unravelled by Sir Rudolph Peters at Oxford. He showed
that vitamin B1 was an essential link in the chain of
reactions involved in the oxidation of carbohydrates in
the body to release energy; to be more precise, it is a
coenzyme.

EXPERIMENTAL RESEARCH

The work of Eijkman is an example of the type of observations that helped in the discovery of the vitamins. Side-by-
side experiments of a new type were being carried out. This
involved feeding laboratory animals on purified diets
instead of their natural foods, observing the changes in
their health, and curing the diseased animals with additional
foods.

For most of the last century it was believed that a diet
consisted of only fuel foods (fats and carbohydrates), with
'albuminous substances' (proteins) and certain mineral
salts. The first evidence of the need for additional factors
came from Lunin in Germany in 1880, when he failed to
rear mice on a diet of casein (purified milk protein), cane
sugar, and water. Yet they lived well on milk alone. He
concluded that there was something in milk other than
casein, fat, milk sugar, and salts.

A similar method was used by a Dutch professor, Pekel-
haring, in 1905. His conclusions would have been the
turning point in the acceptance of the idea of vitamins,
except that his paper, being written in Dutch, was not
read by many other workers until it was translated into
English in 1926. Consequently the honour of being called
the father of vitamins fell to Hopkins at Cambridge. Pekel-
haring fed a group of mice on a baked mixture of casein,
egg white, rice flour, lard, and mineral salts, and within
4 weeks they all died. A similar group survived when only

a small amount of fresh milk was added to the diet. The point was that only a small amount of milk was necessary— there was something present in traces that was essential to life—and this is what we mean by a vitamin.

Hopkins similarly kept rats alive on a purified diet with a few drops of added milk. He showed (Fig. 2.1) how they lost weight until the milk was added, and how the milk-fed group grew only so long as the milk was included. Hopkins expressed his belief, now verified, that scurvy and rickets were caused by 'the absence from the diet of certain unidentified nutrients'.

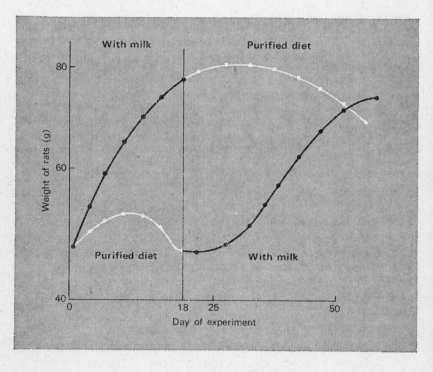

FIG. 2.1. The effects of 3 ml (half-teaspoon) of milk per day on the growth of rats. The animals were fed a purified diet of casein, starch, sugar, and lard. They lost weight (and would eventually have died) unless 3 ml of milk was added to their diet. Milk contains vitamin A, which is needed only in very small amounts (Hopkins, 1912. *J. Physiol.*).

Then followed many years of painstaking research showing that there were several of these factors. First vitamins A and B were discovered, and then B was shown to be a complex of many vitamins; each had to be concentrated, purified, isolated, and chemically identified. This involved the problem of measuring extremely small amounts of vitamins in the presence of very large proportions of other substances like fats, protein, and carbohydrate. A whole new range of chemical, physical, biological, and microbiological techniques was developed to study these small amounts.

This complex task soon involved thousands of research workers from many disciplines in laboratories spread across the world, working with a variety of materials, from natural foods to synthetic chemicals, and using organisms ranging from man to mouse as well as isolated biochemical tissue and micro-organisms. The work multiplied many times as more nutrients were discovered—a score of vitamins, 20 amino acids, and many mineral salts.

The massive collections of findings, revealing what man needs for growth and maintenance of health, are the basic essentials of the science of nutrition. Yet even the task of obtaining this mass of information was relatively easy compared with the job of attempting to relate diets to disease in modern man in his complex environment.

Experimental work, in essence, consists of controlling all the factors except the one under observation, and measuring the changes that follow. But we are now faced with attempting to study the possible effects of diet on heart disease, cancer, brain development, inherited mental disorders, and diseases of the intestine and circulatory system, among others. It is not possible to control all the variables except the one (food) under investigation. We certainly find that the primitive native does not suffer from the same diseases as the inhabitants of London, New York, or Tokyo, and we know that his diet is different. But how do we know whether the diseases are caused by the type or amounts of fat, carbohydrate, or fibre in the diet, or by the hardness of the water, air pollution, traffic noise, the stress of rising prices, or the wearing of synthetic fibre next to the skin?

ENERGY

The normal diet provides protein (needed for the synthesis of tissues), vitamins and minerals (which function as part of the metabolic system), and energy.

Although social customs, habit, and the palatability of the food play a part, the amount of food we eat is largely controlled, through appetite, by our energy needs. Hunger and thirst are the instinctive driving forces; but we have no instinct for selecting nutrients. We can satisfy hunger with almost any food, but we are unable to distinguish between nutritionally good and nutritionally poor foods. We might almost conclude that when we eat to satisfy appetite, the nutrients—that is, the protein, vitamins, and minerals— are more or less accidental contaminants.

The sole function of starch and sugar in the diet and the main function of fats is to provide energy. Protein in excess of that needed for tissue synthesis can also supply energy.

The amount of energy used in normal daily activities can be measured in the form of the heat produced. In the early classical experiments subjects were confined in a calorimeter, which was a small insulated room. All the heat they produced could be measured precisely. Alternatively, since the energy we use comes from the oxidation of food-stuffs, it is possible to calculate the energy indirectly from the oxygen used and the carbon dioxide formed. A second alternative is to measure the energy content of the food eaten. For people who are neither gaining nor losing weight —and despite the number of fat people about, this applies to many of us—the energy coming in from food balances the energy being spent in daily activities.

Starches, sugars, and proteins provide 4 kcal per gram (1 kilocalorie (kcal) = 1 Calorie, a unit which was once in common use). Fats are a more concentrated form of energy and supply 9 kcal per gram. So it is possible, knowing the chemical composition of beans on toast, or strawberries and cream, to calculate how much energy we are consuming. At the same time, if our weight stays constant this is equal to the amount of energy we are using.

Basal metabolism

The first, and for most people the largest, requirement for energy is for the fundamental processes of maintaining body temperature and muscle tone and for keeping the heart beating and the organs functioning. This is termed basal metabolic rate (BMR) and is measured when the subject is resting. It varies with age and sex and is approximately 1 kcal per kilogram (kg) body weight per hour. So an average 65-kg adult (140 lb) will spend about 1600 kcal per day for such basal purposes.

TABLE 2.1

Daily energy balance sheet of a clerk,
weight 66 kg (143 lb) height 1·68 m (5ft 6in)

	Length of time	kilocalories per minute	Total per day kilocalories	megajoules
Sleep	8 hours	1·1	525	2·19
At home				
Light sedentary activity	4 hours	1·48	360	1·51
Washing and dressing	30 min	3·0	90	0·38
Light domestic work	1 hour	3·0	180	0·75
Walking	1 hour	6·6	400	1·67
Gardening	25 min	4·8	120	0·50
Standing	20 min	1·56	30	0·12
At Work				
Sitting activities	3 hours 10 min	1·65	310	1·30
Standing activities	3 hours 40 min	1·9	420	1·76
Walking	12 min	6·6	80	0·33
	Sleeping		525	2·19
	Total working		810	3·40
	Total at home		1180	4·93
	Total		2515	10·52
	(BMR)		(1680)	(7.02)
Energy intake calculated from diet			2620	10·95

In SI units the energy unit is a joule. A megajoule (MJ) is 1 million joules.

The relative importance of BMR in the whole day's energy expenditure is shown by the example of a 65-kg (140 lb) sedentary worker (Table 2.1). He may spend about 2500 kcal in a day, of which BMR accounts for as much as 1600 kcal, or nearly two-thirds of the total. It is rather surprising that even if one stayed in bed all day one would still need two-thirds of one's usual energy intake.

As with all biological measurements there is considerable individual variation in BMR. Two individuals of identical body size may differ by as much as 30 per cent. The rate of metabolism is controlled largely by the thyroid gland, and measurements of BMR are used in the diagnosis of disorders of the thyroid gland and in monitoring their treatment. In cases of over-active thyroid (thyrotoxicosis), the rate may be increased by 100 per cent; it is also increased in fever. In under-activity of the thyroid gland (myxoedema), it may be reduced by 40 per cent.

BMR is constant for any individual, but the rest of his energy expenditure depends on his activity. The breakdown of the energy spent by an individual is given in Table 2.1. If he spent more time walking or gardening instead of sitting, his energy expenditure would go up—but not very dramatically. For example, if he spent twice as long gardening he would use another 120 kcal, which is the amount supplied in one slice of bread and butter. (The correspondingly small amount of body fat used up by increased exercise will be discussed later under the heading of *Obesity*.)

People doing heavy work use more energy than sedentary workers, as indicated in Table 2.2. For example, farmers and coal-miners can use 4000–4500 kcal per day compared with the 2500 kcal used by office workers. Table 2.3 shows the energy used for different types of activity.

One of the most difficult problems of the nutritionist is the variability of his subjects. The figures given in Table 2.2 and 2.3 are the average of measurements carried out on a limited number of subjects. Two people of the same weight, height, sex, and age, doing precisely the same piece of work, such as walking a mile, laying 100 bricks, or playing a round of golf, may use somewhat different amounts of

TABLE 2.2

Daily energy balance sheet of a coal-miner

	kilocalories	megajoules
Sleep	530	2·21
Work	1700	7·09
Remainder	1560	6·50
Total	3780	15·85
(BMR)	(1680)	(7·00)
Energy intake calculated from diet	3990	16·70

TABLE 2.3

Energy expenditure in kilocalories per minute for a 70-kg (154-lb) adult

Daily activities		Maximum efforts	
Washing and dressing	2·6–3·0	Planing hardwood	9·1
Walking: 3·2 km/h	2·9	Shovelling earth	10·3
5 km/h	4·0	Sculling at 97 m/min	11·2
6·5 km/h	5·2	Swimming at 55 m/min	140
Sitting	1·5	Climbing with load	13·2
Sitting and writing	2·0	Skiing up hill	18·6
Driving car	2·8	Walking in loose snow	20·2
Driving motor-cycle	3·4		
Sweeping floor	1·7		
Ironing	4·2		
Polishing floor	4·8		
Recreation		At work (engineering)	
Cycling: 9 km/h	4·5	Light (draughtsmen,	
15 km/h	7·0	drilling, light assembly)	1·8
21 km/h	11·1	Medium (turners, joiners,	
Digging	8·6	toolroom workers)	3·8
Playing tennis	7·1	Heavy (loading, casting,	
Playing football	8·9	machine fitting)	4–7
Cricket—fielding	3·9		
bowling	5·2		
batting	6·0		

From Passmore and Durnin (1955). *Physiol. Rev.* **35**, 801.

energy—and consequently be able to consume different amounts of food without gaining or losing weight.

All that can be done is to measure the amount of energy or nutrients needed by a group of subjects, take the average, and use the figure for assessing the average needs of similar subjects. So we know fairly precisely the needs of the people in a class at school, a home for the elderly, a community, or a nation, and we can plan food production and imports accordingly (always assuming equitable distribution of the food). What we do not know are the needs of any individual in that group.

If people of the same size carrying out the same activities can vary in their needs, how much greater is the range in groups of subjects of different ages and sizes and activities, selected at random? One survey examining the energy intake of several hundred women showed a range from 1000 kcal to 4000 kcal a day. A similar survey for men showed a range from 1000 kcal to 5000 kcal.

If the body weight is not changing, the intake of energy balances the output; so those eating 1000 kcal presumably need only this amount, and those eating 5000 kcal need the large amount. However, if all members of the group are eating the same kind of food, then those at the lower end of the scale are getting one fifth of the vitamins, minerals, and protein than those at the top end—or, perhaps more worrying, less than half of the average. Whether or not, when they need half of the average energy, they also need only half of the average protein, vitamins, and minerals, we do not know. They may be at nutritional risk, but there is no evidence on which to decide this.

Body stores

Most of us eat regularly, and three meals a day is the accepted norm, but some people eat one large meal with little in between, and others eat as many as five small meals a day. In theory, at least, the cells of the body need to be supplied with nutrients and energy continuously, but there is no obvious effect if we miss a meal, or even go

without food for a day. Certainly, people trained to fast
have gone without food for a month or more.

This is possible because there is a considerable store of
energy in the body which maintains a constant flow to the
cells. The liver has about 100 g of stored carbohydrate in
the form of glycogen. The muscles have about 500 g,
which supplies 2400 kcal—enough to last for one day
(Table 2.4).

TABLE 2.4

Available body stores of energy in the adult

Site	Amount in grams	Equivalent in kilocalories	Length of time it will last
Liver—glycogen	100	400	4 hours
Muscles—glycogen	500	2400	1 day
Muscles and skin —protein	6000	25 000	10 days
Fat	11 000 –	100 000 –	1 month –
	100 000	1 000 000	1 year

The protein tissues of the muscles appear to serve to
some extent as a store, both of protein and of energy, since
on prolonged fasting one-third of the muscle proteins can
be broken down without any permanent ill-effects. This
amounts to about 6000 g, providing 25 000 kcal.

By far the largest store of energy in the body, and one
which is too evident in some people, is the fat (more
politely termed adipose tissue). This varies from 11 kg in
a thin person to 100 kg in a fat one. In terms of energy
store this totals between 100 000 kcal, which would last
about 40 days, and 1 000 000 kcal, which would last some
400 days. In fact obese subjects have occasionally been
treated in hospital by complete starvation for periods as
long as a year.

CARBOHYDRATES AND FATS

Starch is the principal ingredient of most diets in all parts
of the world. This is because, with few exceptions, the main

or staple food is a cereal (such as wheat, rice, millet, or maize) or a root crop (such as cassava)—both of which are largely starch. Cereals contain about 75 per cent starch and 10 per cent protein; cassava flour contains 80 per cent starch and 1.5 per cent protein.

In some areas the staple is supplemented with very few other foods, and this one single food can make up two-thirds of the total diet. In the West, although one food dominates the diet (this is wheat in Great Britain), there is a very wide variety of other foods. Surprisingly, the amount of protein eaten does not differ very much between rich and poor countries. It is fat intake that shows the biggest difference, constituting about ten per cent of the diet in developing countries and 40 per cent in the West. The other main difference is that as people become wealthier they replace a large part of the starch by sugar (sucrose). The average diet in Great Britain contains about 12 per cent protein, 40 per cent fat, and over 20 per cent each of starch and sugar.

Fats are present in many foods like milk, meat, cakes, and kippers as well as being obvious in foods such as butter and cooking oils. They serve a number of purposes in the diet as well as in the body. In the diet they often carry much of the flavour of foods; they improve texture; and they assist swallowing by lubricating the food (try eating dry bread). In the body fats serve as a source of energy in the same way as carbohydrates, but since they supply 9 kcal per g compared with 4 kcal per g from carbohydrates, they are a more compact form of food; diets low in fat are more bulky. In addition several of the vitamins (A, D, E, and K) are dissolved in the fat found in foods. One particular type of fat—the so-called essential fatty acids—is, as the name implies, a dietary essential. In fact it was once called vitamin F. So far no one has been found suffering from a deficiency of essential fatty acids: even diets low in fat seem to supply enough.

Two other current ideas about fats will be discussed later. One is the suggestion that animal fats have a detrimental effect on blood cholesterol levels, which may, in turn, be associated with heart disease. The second is that a surplus of essential fatty acids has a beneficial effect.

PROTEINS

The main distinction between living tissues and non-living matter is that the former are made of cells containing protoplasm and a nucleus, both of which are composed of protein. Consequently all living tissues contain protein.

This means that all food—at least in its original state—contains protein. Foods like sugar and fat that have been extracted from their original plant or animal sources do not contain protein, but the starting material (the sugar cane or the olive or the animal tissue) did.

Though we are used to thinking of meat, milk, fish, and so forth as protein foods, which they are, even rhubarb stems and cabbage leaves contain protein, even if only 0.5 per cent and 3 per cent respectively. These relatively poor sources of protein can make a substantial contribution to the diet if enough of them are eaten. We tend to ignore the vegetable marrow as a source of protein, indeed as a source of almost everything since it is 98 per cent water and only 0.4 per cent protein. But the villagers of Nepal can obtain as much as 12 g protein from marrow in a single meal because a 'plateful' may be 3 kg (7 lb). This could be a quarter or a third of their total daily protein intake.

The variety of proteins

Even a quick look at the plant and animal kingdom reveals that there are vast numbers of different proteins in nature. Casein from milk differs obviously from gelatin from connective tissue, or gluten from wheat. These differ again from the proteins in peas or meat and fish. Even within the animal proteins, flesh differs from liver, kidney, and heart. Moreover, each of these is not one protein but is composed of large numbers of different proteins. An organ like the liver contains several hundred different enzymes (all of which are proteins) as well as structural proteins.

Yet all of them are composed of the same 20 amino acids,

and they differ only in the proportions and methods of chemical linkage. A practical analogy is with the letters of the alphabet and words of the language: a quarter of a million words of the English language, plus a larger number in other languages, are all made from 26 letters. Just as repetition of letters and different combinations of so small a number of units can make up so many words, so the 20 amino acids form the vast number of proteins.

Proteins differ enormously in their properties, quite apart from differences in the appearance and taste of food proteins. Just as a word can have a very specific meaning, so a protein can have a specific function; one may be a digestive enzyme, another might be the hormone insulin, and another may carry vitamin A in the blood-stream. Botulinus toxin, of which a fraction of a milligram is fatal to an adult man, is a protein; meat, of which we might eat several hundred grams a day, and wool, which is completely indigestible by man, are also proteins.

During digestion the dietary proteins are chemically broken up, or hydrolysed, to their constituent amino acids. These are absorbed from the small intestine into the blood-stream, and pass to the various organs. Each organ selects the amino acids it requires for resynthesizing into the specific protein of the tissue. This explains how it is possible for the body to make use of such less obvious sources of protein such as lobsters and nuts, as well as the more obvious sources such as meat.

The need for protein

The need for dietary protein is obvious in a child; he is growing and forming new protein tissues. It is not so obvious why an adult, who has finished growing, also needs regular supplies of protein. The need arises because there is a continuous breakdown and rebuilding of all body tissues, termed dynamic equilibrium. It would not be quite correct to term this 'wear and tear', since such a term implies that hard work or excessive usage wears out the tissues faster. In fact the rate of tissue breakdown and renewal is quite constant, and it is independent of physical activity.

The tissues of organs such as liver, kidney, and heart, and the blood plasma proteins are broken down at such a rate that they have a half-life of 10 days. That is, after 10 days half the organ has been replaced, after 20 days half of the remainder has also been replaced, and so on. Muscle, skin, and bone are more stable, and have a half-life of 5 or 6 months. So everyone needs a regular, almost continuous, supply of protein in the diet to maintain his tissues.

When the tissues are broken down, the nitrogen portion of the protein is converted into urea, which is excreted in the urine, and the carbon portion is oxidized and serves as a source of energy. So the loss of nitrogen in the urine is an index of tissue breakdown. There are also small losses in hair and nails and sweat. The total losses provide a method of assessing the amount of dietary protein needed. If the individual is supplied with plenty of energy foods (as carbohydrate and fat), but no protein, then these 'obligatory' losses will be due entirely to the regular turnover in his tissues, and this is the amount that must be replaced. It is still debatable whether supplying protein above these minimal needs is of any benefit. Most palatable diets, certainly of the kind that we are used to eating in the Western world, contain at least twice as much protein as the minimum required. Even cereals, which are the main source of energy foods for a large part of the world, provide about twice the minimum physiological needs for protein if they are eaten in sufficient amounts to satisfy the appetite.

Protein quality

Since the sources of protein range from lobsters to nuts and from rhubarb to cabbage, it would seem that some should be more suitable for the construction of human tissues than others. That is, different proteins must contain the amino acids in proportions more similar or less similar to those found in the human tissues. It is indeed found that proteins differ in their usefulness for this purpose and can be of high or low quality on this basis.

A protein of low quality must be eaten in larger amounts than one of high quality to supply the required amount of the mixture of amino acids. This is certainly true when considering single sources of protein; anyone living solely on wheat protein would need twice as much as his neighbour living on egg protein. However, nobody lives on a single source of protein and all diets, even in developing countries, contain quite a variety of protein foods, so that these differences in quality are averaged out in the diet. Allowance is made for different protein qualities when recommending how much protein should be eaten, but in practice the differences are not very large.

Enough protein?

The amount of protein needed is about 0.5 g per kg body weight, which is about 35 g per day for the average adult. A more useful way of expressing this is as a percentage of the diet rather than as an absolute amount. About 5 per cent of the energy of the diet should come from protein. (If the diet contains 2800 kcal then 140 kcal, which is 5 per cent of this, or 35 g, should come from proteins, and the protein intake should be at least 35 g.)

This method of expressing protein is more useful because there are diets that contain the right percentage of protein but the amount may fall below the 35-g level, because not enough food is eaten. For example, the average diet in Indonesia appears to be very poor since the protein just reaches the 35-g level. However, the diet contains nearly 8 per cent protein. The diet contains the right proportion of protein but not enough food is eaten. The clue lies in the observation that the average intake is only about 2000 kcal. If those people ate more of the same kind of food, say 3000 kcal, they would get 1½ times as much protein—over 50 g. What is needed is more food of the same kind rather than additional protein.

There seems to be a high proportion of protein available to almost every community, even in the developing countries, and there appears to be at most only a few communities where people are getting enough energy but not enough protein.

There is a further point. The body has first call on the energy supplies, and if not enough food is eaten then part of the protein is burned off to supply energy instead of being used for tissue building. So diets that are inadequate in amount are not improved by adding protein alone since this may well be burned off; it is more food that is needed. Babies present more of a problem because their needs for protein are proportionately greater.

Advertising protein

Certain terms like 'bio' and 'electronic' have won a place in the magic of current gimmickry, and in advertising 'protein' has become an in word. Vitamins would seem to be a more likely candidate for magic, since they are so potent in such minute quantities, but advertisers have only recently 'discovered' proteins, and throughout the Western world claims are made for protein content and even protein quality.

There is no legal definition (except in Canada) of terms such as protein-rich, high-protein, or body-building, but to the nutritionist most, if not all, of these claims are un-necessary—there is no evidence that there is any shortage of protein in the countries where people watch television advertisements. In fact it can be argued that in the United States or Great Britain, with the kinds of food available, one would have to be both a knowledgeable nutritionist and a cunning cook to be able to compile a palatable diet that was short of protein. Probably only those who dilute the average diet by substituting half a pound of sweets regularly for their food, or who slim by semi-starvation, might get near the minimum intake of protein.

Protein-rich foods include peas and beans, which are not very popular, and meat, eggs, and milk, which are very popular. One can live perfectly well on only vegetable proteins—half the world does, even if from necessity rather than choice—but most people prefer animal protein foods.

Table 8.1 (p. 135) shows that the production of animal protein makes inefficient use of the land; we could be producing more efficiently (even though we would be less contented) if we became vegetarians.

The emphasis on animal protein as a nutritionally desirable food is based on two points. First, the quality of the protein consumed is usually lower in developing countries than in the West, and a small amount of animal protein foods will supply those amino acids that are in short supply in vegetable foods. Secondly, animal foods also contain other nutrients such as vitamins and iron, which are often in short supply in vegetable diets. This is why many surveys of food consumption list the animal and vegetable proteins separately, and nutritionists often advise increased consumption of animal foods.

SALTS

The other two important ingredients of food are mineral salts and vitamins. The salts are part of the body structure (calcium and phosphate form the skeleton, and iron is an ingredient of the blood), and they play a part in the functioning of the enzyme systems which affect all the body processes. These minerals are magnesium, manganese, copper, zinc, chloride, sulphate, and many others in trace amounts. Apart from iron and iodine, all the minerals are widespread and are needed in such small amounts that dietary deficiencies are rare.

VITAMINS

Fats and carbohydrates are seen and handled daily, examples of proteins can be provided by egg white and milk casein, and mineral salts are exemplified by ordinary table salt, but vitamins are difficult to visualize since they are present in such small, invisible amounts. Only a few milligrams are present in thousands of grams of food. Therefore, apart from the pure crystalline vitamins used in the laboratory and factory, they are not seen and handled by the ordinary consumer.

In the earlier days of nutrition research, a vitamin was recognized by its absence. It was said that vitamin D was the vitamin whose absence caused rickets and that vitamin B1 was the vitamin whose absence caused beri-beri. In fact there was an old 'music-hall' definition describing a vitamin as 'something that is fatal to you if you don't eat it'. It is only when the detailed biochemical function of the vitamin is unravelled that it can be described in positive terms. So now we can say that not only does the absence of vitamin B1 give rise to beri-beri, but that its function in the cells of the body is to act as a coenzyme in the oxidation of glucose and other foodstuffs to provide energy. The biochemical function of most of the vitamins of the B group has been discovered, but we still do not know in detail the functions of vitamins A, D, and E, and there are many gaps in our knowledge of other vitamins.

Vitamin deficiencies

Scurvy, rickets, beri-beri, and pellagra are each the outward sign of a deficiency of a specific vitamin, and these diseases are found in many parts of the world because of poor diets. There are many possible causes apart from the obvious one of shortage of the vitamin itself. The vitamin may require other dietary ingredients before it can be used. For example, a deficiency of vitamin A can arise even when the diet supplies enough of the vitamin if there is not enough fat to assist its absorption from the intestine, or not enough protein to transport it in the blood-stream. Diseases that affect the intestine reduce the amount of vitamin absorbed. There are antivitamin substances in some foods that antagonize the effects of the nutrient; and various diseases can increase the requirements for a vitamin or, indeed, for other nutrients as well, making inadequate what was normally a good diet.

When the vitamin deficiency is severe the disease is readily diagnosed. When it is mild the signs are not so clearly defined, and it becomes extremely difficult to be certain that there is a shortage. For example, pellagra, which arises from a shortage of niacin, may be diagnosed from the appearance of the skin (*pelle agra* means rough skin). At times even experts have been misled when studying people from mountain communities who were regularly exposed to the sun and the wind—their rough skin was due to weather, not a vitamin deficiency. Another problem arises because some of the signs are not specific for one particular vitamin shortage—a smooth, glazed tongue (glossitis) may be found in deficiencies of niacin, vitamin B2, B12, folic acid, or iron. Furthermore, there can be very few diets that are short of only one nutrient. They are usually poor in many respects, so that signs of several different shortages may show up at the same time.

Of the 14 vitamins it is possible to distinguish those which present nutritional problems because there are communities suffering from dietary deficiencies, and those of more medical interest, because they usually show up in connection with a disease rather than a dietary shortage. The 6 vitamins of greatest nutritional interest are A, B1, B2, C, D, and nicotinic acid (niacin). Vitamin deficiencies will be discussed in more detail as each vitamin is dealt with in turn.

Vitamin nomenclature

The names of the vitamins are somewhat confusing since they have not only letters, numbers, and names but also in some instances more than one name. This confusion arose during the course of their discovery. The first vitamin to be isolated was called, logically, vitamin A; it was soluble in fat but not in water. A short time later it became clear that there was another accessory food factor which was water-soluble, so that the names fat-soluble vitamin A and water-soluble vitamin B arose. Subsequently the vitamin B was shown to be a mixture of several factors, and hence the vitamin Bs had numbers attached; now we have vitamins B1, B2, B6, and B12. There are now altogether 20 substances that have been called vitamins, of which 14 are well established. The commonly used names of the different vitamins are shown in Table 2.5.

TABLE 2.5

Vitamin nomenclature

Vitamin A	Retinol in animal food; carotene in vegetables
Vitamin B1	Thiamin
Vitamin B2	Riboflavin
Niacin	Nicotinic acid and nicotinamide (niacin and niacinamide in the United States)
Vitamin C	Ascorbic acid
Vitamin D	Cholecalciferol
Vitamin E	Tocopherols
Folacin	Folic acid
Vitamin B6	Pyridoxine, pyridoxal, pyridoxamine
Vitamin B12	Cyanocobalamin

The multiplicity of names arose because different laboratories discovered the same vitamin and gave it different names. Vitamin B2 was found independently in milk (and called lactoflavin), in egg (and called ovoflavin), and in liver (and called hepatoflavin). The name finally agreed upon was riboflavin. Another oddity arose from the fact that some of the vitamins were known as chemical compounds many years before they were shown to have any physiological activity. So nicotinic acid and carotene were in fact discovered many years before the word vitamin was coined.

Assay methods

The nutritionist sets the analyst quite a problem when he wants to be able to measure, not merely to detect, the amount of a vitamin in a food or in the body. These measurements must be made of the order of one part of a vitamin in a million parts of food. Wholemeal bread contains 0·3 mg of vitamin B6 per 100 g bread, a concentration of 3 parts per million; biotin (vitamin H) is present in 1 part per 50 million of bread.

The obvious method of measuring a vitamin is to find

how much it takes to cure the disease in animals that have
been deprived of the vitamin in question. For example, how
much of a food containing the vitamin is needed to cure
rickets compared with a known dose of the pure vitamin?
In this way vitamin C can be assayed by its curative effect
of scurvy in guinea-pigs, and vitamin A by its growth
promotion of vitamin A deficient rats.

Such biological methods are expensive, they may take
several weeks, and they are not very accurate because of the
individual variation of the test animals. They have been
largely replaced by physical and chemical methods which
depend on the specific physical or chemical properties of
the vitamin, so specific that almost no other substance
gives the same reaction. So now it is relatively easy to measure
the amount of a vitamin in a food or a body tissue.

Vitamin A: retinol (animal foods) and carotene (plant foods)

Vitamin A has a number of functions in the body; it is
concerned with growth, with maintaining the moist condition of the soft mucous tissues that line the respiratory
tract and other passages in the body, and with night-vision.
The first sign of a shortage is the inability to see in dim
light, known as night-blindness.

When one goes from bright light into a dimly lit room,
it is difficult to see anything at first. Then after a few
minutes the eyes become adapted and things become
clearer. This is because a vitamin A–protein compound
called visual purple is necessary for night-vision. It is
'bleached out' in bright light and takes a few minutes to be
resynthesized. When vitamin A is in short supply, a rare
occurrence in this country, the eyes adapt more slowly or
not at all—this is night-blindness.

At a later stage of vitamin A deficiency the tear ducts of
the eyes become blocked and the conjunctiva becomes dry
and inflamed (xerophthalmia is Greek for dry eyes); with
a prolonged shortage of the vitamin the cornea becomes
ulcerated (keratomalacia) and blindness results. Vitamin A
deficiency is a common cause of blindness in children in

some parts of the world, including India and the Middle East.

Vitamin A is found in foods in two forms, as carotene in plants and as retinol in animal foods such as milk and liver. The deep orange colour of carrots and red palm oil is due to the large amount of carotene present. All green leaves contain carotene but the colour is masked by the green chlorophyll. Apricots, peaches, papaya, and yellow melons owe their colour to carotene. Since the vitamin is fat-soluble and is found in milk, it is present in a more concentrated form in the butter and cheese made from the milk; it is added to margarine in many countries. With so much present in our common foods, vitamin A deficiency is extremely rare in this country.

In the body carotene is converted into retinol and stored in the liver, so this is one of the nutrients that need not be consumed daily but could, if necessary, be taken every few weeks. It is possible to hold very large stores in the liver, and in areas where a deficiency is common children can be treated with massive doses, enough to last for months or even a year or so. Storage in the liver also explains why animal liver, cod liver oil, and halibut liver oil are rich sources of the vitamin—so long as the animals and fish consume more than they need.

B vitamins: B1 (thiamin), B2 (riboflavin), and niacin

Both vitamins B1 and B2 have a number as well as a specific chemical name, but niacin never had a letter or number attached to it. It is found in foods in two forms, as the free acid, nicotinic acid, and as the amide, nicotinamide. Both are equally useful to the body. The official nomenclature uses the name niacin as a general description for both compounds, in the same way as vitamin A is the general description for both carotene and retinol. It was once called vitamin PP (pellagra-preventative), and this name has been used on food labels since it is more informative than the chemical name.

These three members of the B group of vitamins have

several features in common: they all take part in the same
set of metabolic reactions, they are often found together
in food, and they have a common history since they were
isolated from a mixture originally called vitamin B.

They function as part of the enzyme systems in the series
of reactions involved in the oxidation of carbohydrates,
fats, and proteins whereby energy is released for use in the
tissues. Each stage of the twenty or so reactions is carried
out by a specific enzyme, and some of these stages require
the assistance of a coenzyme made from one of these
vitamins.

Clinically the absence of each B vitamin leads to a specific and different disorder. Lack of thiamin results in beri-
beri, a disease of the nervous system which can lead to
heart failure. A shortage of niacin leads to pellagra, a disease
of the skin, digestive system, and brain. A shortage of riboflavin has no specific name but is recognized by the cracking
of the skin at the corners of the mouth, a smooth tongue,
and changes in the lips. None of these disorders occurs,
other than in very exceptional circumstances, in the Western world, but all are common in countries that live pre-
dominantly on white rice or maize.

Beri-beri is a national problem where the diet is restricted
in variety and contains no foods rich in thiamin. It is
associated with the consumption of polished rice, because
this often comprises 60–80 per cent of the diet and contains
little of the vitamin. The tragic part is that the original
brown rice is a rich source of all the B vitamins, but people
prefer their rice white and polished, a process in which
the germ is removed together with the outer layers of bran.
The principle is very similar to the milling of whole wheat
to white flour—a product that is preferred in Western
countries—which would also give rise to vitamin deficiencies were it not that Western diets include many other
foods that supply the missing vitamins. In addition, some
wheat-eating countries enrich their flour with B vitamins,
but there is no enrichment in most countries where rice
is the staple food because of the lack of technology and
facilities.

Pellagra illustrates the complexities of the study of nutrition. It was first described by Casals in Spain in 1735 and was also common at that time in Italy. It was associated with maize eating, and was thought to be caused by a toxin. Nearly 200 years later Goldberger in the United States realized that pellagrins lived on diets poor in protein, and he thought that this was the cause of the disease. Later the cause was found to be a vitamin deficiency. In 1937 when the complex story of the B vitamins was being unravelled, nicotinic acid was isolated from yeast and shown to cure pellagra.

Two later findings showed that Goldberger was partly correct. First, it was found that there is niacin in maize but that it is present in a chemically combined form that is not available to the body. Secondly, the amino acid, tryptophan, was found to be in short supply in maize (and, of course, in any diet that is short of protein). This amino acid can be converted into nicotinic acid in the body. So diets short of both the vitamin and the amino acid cause pellagra, and this is why the disease is widespread in most communities that subsist on maize. An interesting exception is Mexico: the Mexicans soak their maize in lime-water overnight before making it into tortillas. This process liberates the nicotinic acid from its chemical binding, so that it becomes biologically available.

Thiamin and niacin occur richly in cereal germ together with a small amount of riboflavin, which occurs richly in milk and liver with some of the other two vitamins. All three are found in smaller amounts in vegetables, nuts, beans, and other foods.

All three are soluble in water, and some can be lost in cooking simply by being washed out into the water. Sulphur dioxide, often used as a food preservative, destroys thiamin very rapidly but has no effect on the other two B vitamins. It is used to keep ready-peeled potatoes and chips white, so some of the vitamin (at least in the outer layers) is destroyed in these convenience products. It can also be used to preserve minced-meat products such as sausages, and here all the thiamin is rapidly destroyed.

The loss of the vitamin may be considered a price worth paying for protection from a potential source of food poisoning.

Vitamin C (ascorbic acid)

The result of a prolonged shortage of vitamin C is scurvy. As discussed earlier, scurvy was historically associated with sailors on long sea voyages because vitamin C is mostly obtained from fresh fruits and vegetables, which were unavailable away from land. Scurvy is still occasionally found even in well-fed countries where some people, such as bachelors living alone and elderly persons, cannot be bothered to peel potatoes or prepare vegetables and do not eat fruit. It can be largely washed out of vegetables like chopped cabbage during cooking, and is quickly destroyed by air in vegetables that are kept hot; thus poor cooking practice can also lead to a shortage.

The general function of vitamin C is to keep the connective tissue, including the cells of the walls of the blood capillaries, in a proper state of repair. The symptoms of scurvy follow from a breakdown of connective tissue, causing small patches of bleeding under the skin and swollen and bleeding gums and making wounds slow to heal.

Unlike the other vitamins, a dietary supply of vitamin C is needed by only a few species. These include man, monkey, and the guinea-pig, together with rather exotic animals like the fruit-eating bat and the red-vented bul-bul bird. All other species can synthesize their own ascorbic acid.

This has led to some confusion in deciding how much vitamin C we should consume. Animal and human experiments suggest that 30 mg per day is adequate for an adult, and this is the figure recommended both in Great Britain and by the World Health Organization. However, animals that synthesize their own vitamin C have higher concentrations of it in their blood. This led the National Research Council of America to recommend first 70 mg, then 60 mg, and more recently 45 mg per day. To add to the confusion, the Russian authorities recommend 100 mg per day.

Nearly all fruits and vegetables contain vitamin C and some, such as oranges, blackcurrants, and soft fruits, are so rich in it that a portion once a week would supply enough. In Great Britain the average individual obtains a quarter of his vitamin C from potatoes. The proportion is even higher in winter, because the average intake of potatoes here is high and the average British intake of fruits and other vegetables is the lowest in Europe.

Vitamin D (cholecalciferol)

Vitamin D has the unusual feature of being manufactured in the body—in the skin under the influence of sunlight—and so need not be consumed. A shortage results in rickets, a disease that was common for several hundred years in Northern Europe where the sunshine is usually somewhat limited. Vitamin D is found in some foods (including eggs, fatty fish, and butter), but there are not many foods that provide a reasonable amount so we generally have to rely on sunlight for part of our supply of the vitamin.

Rickets occurs in young children and is due to poor bone formation. Vitamin D assists in the absorption of calcium from food into the blood-stream, and also assists the deposition of calcium to form bone. There is an equivalent disease in adults, called osteomalacia, caused by the loss of calcium from the bones. This occurs in some parts of the world in women who have repeated pregnancies and live on a poor diet. The poor diet means that the demands of the foetus for calcium to form its bones are met by taking calcium from the mother's bones; the women concerned often stay indoors for a large part of the time and so do not receive the ultraviolet light needed for synthesis of the vitamin in the skin. For the same reason osteomalacia is found in Western countries among the housebound elderly people who live on a poor diet.

Rickets was extremely common in poor areas of the cities

of Great Britain until the 1940s. It has now largely disappeared for a number of reasons. Many babies receive
cod-liver oil or other preparations rich in vitamin D. The
vitamin is added to many baby foods and to margarine.
Smoke-free zones in our cities have led to larger amounts
of ultraviolet light reaching our skin. Finally, compared
with earlier generations, it is much commoner for us to
expose our bodies to sunshine.

Other vitamins: B6 (pyridoxine), B12, folic acid, panto-thenic acid

The vitamins described so far are those of major nutritional
interest. There are another dozen vitamins of lesser nutritional importance in the sense that shortages of them
are relatively rare and may arise only in special circumstances where the need is greater than usual or from disease.
For example, there are no communities where a deficiency
of vitamin B6 (pyridoxine) or folic acid is common; all
diets, even in poorly fed areas, provide enough for the
average person. However, there are cases of deficiencies in
pregnant women because of the additional needs of the
growing foetus.

It was a set of special circumstances that brought to light,
as recently as 1954, the fact that vitamin B6 is essential for
human beings. It had been shown to be essential for rats
in 1926, and it had been purified in 1938, but there was
no evidence that human beings needed it. In 1954 a special
variety of milk that involved excessive heat treatment was
put on the market for feeding babies in the United States.
The infants developed seizures similar to those of epilepsy,
which were traced to the destruction of vitamin B6 by
the heating process.

Another vitamin, B12, is essential to man, but dietary
deficiencies are extremely rare. Normal, healthy people
nearly always obtain enough from their diets, but some
people suffer from an inability to absorb the vitamin and
eventually develop pernicious anaemia. Pantothenic acid
deficiency is very rare.

Vitamins in food technology

Vitamin C is widely used in the food industry as a chemical reducing agent. It is added to fruit juices to prevent a darkening of the colour, to pickled meats such as ham to maintain the red colour, and to flour used in bread-making. The total amount of vitamin C synthesized in factories throughout the world is about 20 000 tonnes a year, mostly for technological rather than nutritional purposes. This amount is just about enough to satisfy the needs of every man, woman, and child in the world!

The form of vitamin A found in plants, carotene, and several similar compounds that are reddish in colour are used as food colouring—the nutritional value is a bonus to the consumer. On the other hand, palm oil, which is deep orange–red because of its concentration of carotene, has to be bleached and the vitamin destroyed because world markets demand a pale-coloured oil for making margarine and cooking fat mixtures.

Vitamin E (tocopherol) is a natural preservative found in many vegetable oils. It is sometimes added to fats and fatty foods as an antioxidant.

Apart from these technological uses, vitamins are, of course, added to some foods like margarine, bread, and baby foods for nutritional enrichment.

Extra-large intake and overdose of vitamins

When advertisers claimed that their particular vitamin would prevent an ailment, the truth was that it would do so only if the ailment arose in the first place because of a shortage of that vitamin. Certainly a superfluity of any vitamin does no good; once there is 'enough', then by definition more cannot do any good—enough is enough.

There are some examples where a phenomenally large dose has a specific effect, but these doses are so great that they are outside the range of the definition of vitamins, which function in minute amounts. In large quantities the substances have a pharmacological, or drug, action.

In recent years there have been suggestions, subject to much controversy, that vitamin C at a 100 times the vitamin dosage level prevents the common cold. Such treatment has been glorified by the term 'megavitamin therapy', but since the daily dose is as great as the entire body content of the vitamin, it is acting as a drug and the effects, even if true, are outside the range of normal diets and normal vitamin function.

Large doses of vitamins are used in certain clinical conditions, quite apart from treatment of vitamin deficiencies. For example, nicotinic acid is sometimes used to dilate the peripheral blood-vessels in the treatment of certain vascular disorders. It also stimulates the secretion of acid in the stomach. Large doses of vitamin B12 have been used to treat various nerve disorders, and vitamin B6 has been used in the treatment of radiation sickness and the nausea of early pregnancy. Large doses of vitamin D, about 1000 times the vitamin requirement, used to be given for tuberculosis of the skin. These high dose levels are quite different from the one-time hope that vitamins were the elixir of life and that superabundant doses of vitamins would produce superabundant health—they do not.

While there is no known benefit from taking extra vitamins, except as an insurance against not getting enough, the possibility of harm arising from excessive amounts must be considered. Overdosage is unlikely with vitamin C and the B vitamins, since these are water-soluble and any surplus is quickly excreted in the urine, although there can be a temporary local concentration. One exception is nicotinic acid; a few hundred milligrams, which is about 10 times the daily requirement, can cause an intense flushing of the skin of the face and neck. This does not appear to be harmful, and it is used, as mentioned above, to dilate the blood-vessels. Overdosage with nicotinic acid occurred in Great Britain in the 1960s when butchers sprinkled a mixture of nicotinic acid and vitamin C onto raw meat to maintain the original bright red colour. It was used in excessive amounts, and its sale for such purposes was banned.

Vitamins A and D are stored in the body, and cases of overdosage are very occasionally reported. It appears to have been traditional for many years to warn polar explorers against eating polar-bear liver, although it was not known why. In 1944 the tale was put to the test by feeding polar bear liver to rats, when it did indeed, prove toxic. Separation of the various ingredients of the liver led eventually to the isolation of the toxic portion, which turned out to be retinol (vitamin A). The polar bear lives on fish, whose livers are rich in retinol, and on mosses, which contain carotene, so it builds up large stores of vitamin A.

Such poisoning has also been reported from eating halibut liver, which is also very rich in retinol. In 1970 a group of fishermen caught a halibut that was 2 m long, and they sat down to a meal of grilled liver, eating amounts varying from 25 g to 300 g each. Within 5 hours they were ill, and after 24 hours their skin began to peel.

These are rare and unusual cases, with unusual foods. The greater risk is that reported of a number of babies who were given, by mistake, large doses of retinol in medicinal preparations. Medicinal preparations contain very much more retinol than is ever likely to occur in any foods (apart from polar-bear liver and halibut liver). Indeed, the death was reported in 1974 of a man who took enormous doses of vitamin A in capsules, against medical advice. (He also drank a gallon of carrot juice every day, but this is harmless.)

A more serious situation occurred with vitamin D. This arose not so much from overdosage as from the excessive sensitivity of some babies. In 1952 a new disease was described, idiopathic (meaning 'of unknown origin') hypercalcaemia (high blood levels of calcium). The symptoms were loss of appetite, vomiting, constipation, and alteration of the facial appearance; the disease could be fatal. It was believed to be due to excessive sensitivity in some babies—only 70 cases were reported—to the vitamin D enriched foods that are well tolerated by the vast majority. Since that time the amount of vitamin D added to baby foods has been reduced, and the difficult course must be steered between rickets (from a shortage of vitamin D), on the one side, and idiopathic hypercalcaemia on the other.

3

How much is enough?

Every nutrient (defined as a dietary essential) is required by all human beings—and usually by many other species as well. The amount required, however, varies with different individuals, so the question, 'How much is needed?' is more difficult to answer than 'What is needed?' For many nutrients, particularly the vitamins, the quantity is arrived at from three directions: extrapolation from animal experiments, observations of human populations, and experiments on human subjects.

Determining the needs of animals can be done with reasonable precision, although there is always considerable individual variation. For example, one of the principal effects of a shortage of vitamin A is the failure to grow, so that the optimum intake of vitamin A is the amount needed for maximum growth. A group of animals is fed on a diet devoid of the vitamin, and thus the body reserves are gradually depleted. When the reserves are nearly all used up, growth begins to slow down and finally stops (Fig. 3.1). If the vitamin is not provided at this time the animals lose weight and eventually die. Small doses will maintain weight or allow slow growth; increasing doses will increase the growth until this reaches a maximum. At this stage, the animal is considered to be receiving the 'required amount' of vitamin A. Animals vary individually, so the final figure for the required amount is the average requirement of a group of animals.

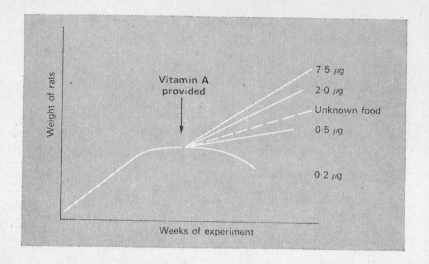

FIG. 3.1. A biological assay of vitamin A. The animals grow without a dietary supply of vitamin A for 4–5 weeks because they have stores in the liver. When the stores are depleted they stop growing, and will die of vitamin A deficiency unless some is provided. 0·5 μg per day just restores growth.

The next problem is to scale up the figure for human beings. Depending on the type of nutrient, this may be by the multiplication by relative body weights, body weight minus fat, relative surface areas of the two bodies, ratio of food intakes, or some other factor. When the specific function of the nutrient is known, this can be used as the basis for selecting the method of scaling up. For example, since vitamin B1 is concerned with energy release from foods, the amounts required are related to energy usage, and multiplying the rat requirements for the vitamin by the relative food intake of man will provide a reasonable approximation to man's requirements of the vitamin. If the vitamin is concerned with protein metabolism then scaling up may be related to the amount of protein eaten or to the relative amounts of body protein.

The second—historically the first—method of deciding

nutrient requirements is the observation of population groups. If, for example, scurvy is observed in people consuming 5 mg of vitamin C per day, but not in those consuming 10 mg per day, then the requirements are somewhere between the two figures.

The third method is to render human volunteers deficient by feeding them a diet devoid of the nutrient, and then to find how much of the nutrient is needed to cure or prevent the deficiency symptoms. It is hoped that the results of all three methods will agree reasonably well.

It is at this stage that the greatest problem arises. The investigation provides information about the requirements of the group of subjects in the experiment, and the figures always lie within a certain range, that is, some people need more of the nutrient than others need, even when they are the same size and engaged in the same activities. This means that we know only the average needs and cannot forecast the precise needs of any individual, unless he happened to be one of the experimental group.

The collected results of all the human experiments that have been carried out on any particular nutrient can be plotted as a distribution curve (Fig. 3.2). About the same number of people require less than the average as require more; that is, to the statistician this is approximately a 'normal' distribution curve. The curve suggests that a very small number of people have extremely high needs and a very small number have very low needs, with the vast majority falling in the range between 20 per cent above and 20 per cent below the average (statistically this is 2 standard deviations). So when deciding how much of a nutrient *should be* consumed by people in general—a figure termed the recommended daily intake (R.D.I.) or allowance (R.D.A.)—we select the higher value (that is the average plus 20 per cent). This means that while the average person would get 20 per cent more than he needs, and those with very low requirements would get 40 per cent more than they need, those people with high needs would get enough. So, in general, the recommended daily intake is the *average*

TABLE 3·1

Recommended daily intakes of energy and nutrients for Great Britain

Age	Occupational category	Body weight (kg)	Energy (kcal)	Protein† (g)	Thiamin (mg)	Riboflavin (mg)	Nicotinic acid (mg)	Ascorbic acid (mg)	Vitamin A (µg)	Vitamin D (µg)	Calcium (mg)	Iron (mg)
Boys and girls												
0 up to 1 year		7·3	800	20	0·3	0·4	5	15	450	10	600	6
1 up to 2 years		11·4	1200	30	0·5	0·6	7	20	300	10	500	7
2 up to 3 years		13·5	1400	35	0·6	0·7	8	20	300	10	500	7
3 up to 5 years		16·5	1600	40	0·6	0·8	9	20	300	10	500	8
5 up to 7 years		20·5	1800	45	0·7	0·9	10	20	300	2·5	500	8
7 up to 9 years		25·1	2100	53	0·8	1·0	11	20	400	2·5	500	10
Boys												
9 up to 12 years		31·9	2500	63	1·0	1·2	14	25	575	2·5	700	13
12 up to 15 years		45·5	2800	70	1·1	1·4	16	25	725	2·5	700	14
15 up to 18 years		61·0	3000	75	1·2	1·7	19	30	750	2·5	600	15
Girls												
9 up to 12 years		33·0	2300	58	0·9	1·2	13	25	575	2·5	700	13
12 up to 15 years		48·6	2300	58	0·9	1·4	16	25	725	2·5	700	14
15 up to 18 years		56·1	2300	58	0·9	1·4	16	30	750	2·5	600	15

Men											
18 up to 35 years											
Sedentary	65	2700	68	1·1	1·7	18	30	750	2·5	500	10
Moderately active		3000	75	1·2	1·7	18	30	750	2·5	500	10
Very active		3600	90	1·4	1·7	18	30	750	2·5	500	10
35 up to 65 years											
Sedentary	65	2600	65	1·0	1·7	18	30	750	2·5	500	10
Moderately active		2900	73	1·2	1·7	18	30	750	2·5	500	10
Very active		3600	90	1·4	1·7	18	30	750	2·5	500	10
65 up to 75 years Assuming a sedentary life	63	2350	59	0·9	1·7	18	30	750	2·5	500	10
75 and over	63	2100	53	0·8	1·7	18	30	850	2·5	500	10
Women											
18 up to 55 years Most occupations	55	2200	55	0·9	1·3	15	30	750	2·5	500	12
Very active		2500	63	1·0	1·3	15	30	750	2·5	500	12
55 up to 75 years Assuming a sedentary life	53	2050	51	0·8	1·3	15	30	750	2·5	500	10
75 and over	53	1900	48	0·7	1·3	15	30	750	2·5	500	10
Pregnancy: 2nd and 3rd trimester	60	2400	60	1·0	1·6	18	60	750	10	1200	15
Lactation	68	2700	68	1·1	1·8	·21	60	1200	10	1200	15

From the Department of Health and Social Security, 1969.

† Recommended intakes calculated as providing 10 per cent of energy.

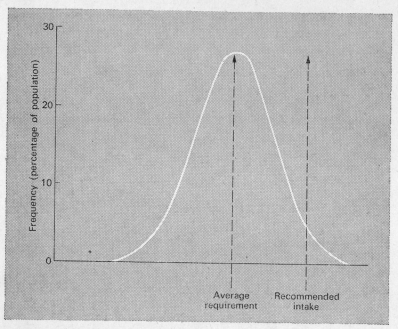

FIG. 3.2. The average requirements and recommended daily intakes of nutrients. Individuals differ in their dietary needs: some require more and others less than the average. Generally, the highest values are 20 per cent greater than the average; so an intake 20 per cent greater than the average requirements will cover the needs of nearly everyone (statistically 97 per cent of the population). This increased figure then becomes the recommended intake.

requirement plus 20 per cent. These are the values established for different ages and sexes in Table 3.1.

As stated above there are a very small number of people whose needs are even greater than average plus 20 per cent; in theory these amount to only 2·5 per cent of the total population—at least, if the distribution curve as shown in Fig. 3.2 is accurate. In other words, the R.D.I. will cover the needs of 97·5 per cent of the population. This is a theoretical figure; in practice we do not seem to find the 2·5 per cent of people with such high needs. However, this piece of mathematics has given rise to the pedantic statement which appears in both nutrition books and official reports that the amounts recommended will "take care of the needs of the greater part of the population'.

DIAGNOSIS OF MALNUTRITION

The figures of R.D.I. shown in Table 3.1 are used both to plan menus and to assess the nutrient intake of groups of people in the community. If the meal on average supplies the R.D.I., then (97·5 per cent of) the population will be adequately nourished. Conversely, if surveys of food intake show that the average intake falls below this figure, then there is cause for concern—the needs of those with high requirements may not be satisfied. The figures in Table 3.1, however, cannot be applied to individuals, since they are group averages. If an individual is consuming less than R.D.I. it may mean nothing, as his needs could be 20 per cent or even 40 per cent below R.D.I. Only if his intake is more than 40 per cent below would he seem to be at risk.

In comparison with the exact sciences it may appear imprecise to say that such an individual would 'seem' to be suffering from malnutrition. You may think that if he is taking less than the needs of the lower end of the scale then surely he must be suffering from malnutrition. The problem is that it is extremely difficult to recognize mild deficiencies of any nutrients; moreover, it is possible that, for some nutrients (certainly for energy and often for protein), the subject adapts to the lower level and therefore shows no deficiency signs. Certainly when a subject has spongy and bleeding gums and his teeth fall out, and at the same time he has patches of haemorrhage under the skin and into the joints, there is little difficulty in diagnosing scurvy. But we do not know what happens under conditions of mild deficiency.

The gradually merging states of undernutrition are shown in Fig. 3.3. By definition the optimum diet produces optimum health, body stores are full, and coenzymes are functioning with maximum efficiency. If intake is reduced below R.D.I., even 40 per cent below, there is no immediate effect; body stores will begin to be depleted, but in the

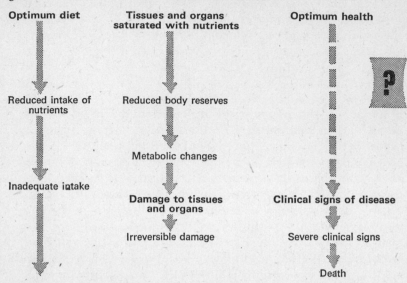

FIG. 3.3. The merging states of nutrition.

early stages this cannot be considered harmful. Nevertheless, the nutritionist regards reduced intake as an early warning sign.

The next stage in undernutrition is reached when the intake has been low long enough for the stores to be depleted; but this may not affect the functioning of the tissues in any way. It is, however, regarded as a serious matter if an individual's stores are low. For example, the well-fed Englishman carries 2 years' supply of vitamin A in his liver; logically, if he had no stores and was guaranteed a regular daily supply of his needs there would be no cause for alarm. Yet nutritionists like to see a good store, presumably on the 'rainy day' principle. So, if an inadequate intake is an early warning sign, low stores present a serious problem.

At a later stage of undernutrition there would be reduced efficiency of metabolic processes, what was termed in earlier days a 'biochemical lesion'. There would not yet be any external sign, that is, no clinical signs of any disorder. All these stages are reversible as soon as the deficient nutrient is supplied.

The next stage occurs when the shortage of a nutrient is great enough to cause functional damage and changes in the tissue or organ—producing the clinical signs such as dermatitis, cracking of the lips, or tiny patches of bleeding at the base of the hair follicles. This state is still reversible. The final stage of undernutrition is irreversible damage and, since nutrients such as vitamins and minerals are essential to life, ultimately death ensues.

So, as Fig. 3.3 shows, there is a gradual merging of conditions when an individual's diet is deficient in a nutrient, and it is impossible to draw a sharp line between adequate and inadequate nutritional status. The problem is similar to the old philosophy question, 'how many hairs make a beard?'

An example of the problem is the annual measurement of food consumption undertaken by second-year nutrition students at Queen Elizabeth College. Every item of food eaten or drunk in a week is weighed—a long and laborious process. Of a class of 30, the intakes of vitamin A ranged from 400 μg to 4000 μg (a microgram is one-millionth of a gram). Since the recommended daily intake is 750 μg, some students were getting less than the minimum requirements (less than 60 per cent R.D.I.)—yet none showed any signs of deficiency.

There are several possible explanations. First, almost every assessment of nutrient intake, even a complete week's weighing, makes use of average food-composition tables, and only rarely does anyone analyse the actual food eaten. So the vitamin A intake from a particular helping of food could be higher (or lower) than the calculated figure. Secondly, the week of measurement may not be representative of the regular food intake of an individual. Thirdly, since the precise requirements of only very few people have ever been measured, it is possible that some people, including those consuming only 400 μg on average per day, may have needs below those reported. Fourthly, low intakes may lead to adaptation. Fifthly, the students may be taking less than they should and their liver reserves may be falling, so that if their deficient diets continue they should show signs of deficiency in future. It would presumably take many years to show such a deficiency if the normally well-fed person has 2 years' supply of vitamin A. Such a person—say, one who was given cod-liver oil in childhood—could survive with no outward signs at all for 4 years if he consumed half his needs, or for 8 years if he consumed three-quarters of his needs.

It is therefore very difficult to decide whether an individual is at risk, even if he is consuming less than the nutritionist thinks he should be. The results may develop slowly and therefore be long delayed. When the subject does eventually become deficient it is more than likely that another disorder such as infection will supervene, so that if death does result it will not be diagnosed as being primarily due to a nutritional deficiency.

A geriatrician put the problem in a nutshell when he said, 'The three well-known signs of niacin deficiency, namely the disease pellagra, are dementia, diarrhoea, and dermatitis. If an elderly patient is suffering from confusion, faecal incontinence and scaliness of the skin of the legs, is this a mild vitamin deficiency?' The question cannot be answered, but it illustrates the difficulties facing nutritionists.

NUTRITION SURVEYS

It is often important to ascertain the nutritional state of communities in developing countries. This is a long, laborious, and expensive undertaking because it involves three major investigations.

Food intake is measured to see whether this falls below recommended levels. To do this properly the food consumed by each individual in the selected cross-section of the community should be measured for a week, and the measurements repeated 2 or even 3 times during different seasons of the year. In practice, such measurements are abbreviated to a single week, or a rough approximation is made from the food purchases of the whole family. Such investigations may yield no firm conclusions, unless the intake of one or more nutrients is extremely low.

Secondly, clinical examinations are carried out. These will certainly reveal any serious nutritional deficiencies that may be present. Alternatively the clinical signs may be mild and non-specific, but they may lend support to the suspicions aroused in the food-measurement investigations.

The third investigation is of biochemical function. This will indicate the amounts of nutrients in the blood or tissues, or provide some biochemical index related to nutrients. Firm conclusions cannot be drawn from this type of test alone, since it can reveal only that the levels of a nutrient in an individual are below average—they may even be normal for that particular individual.

However, the evidence from all three sets of tests can point to a deficiency of a specific nutrient. The final conclusion can be drawn if, after the missing nutrient is supplied, the clinical signs disappear, the biochemical indicators return to the standard values, and there is some resulting benefit to the health of the subject.

The results of such surveys are certainly reliable and meaningful when applied to communities. When polished rice is the staple diet and beri-beri presents a public health problem, this will clearly show in each of the investigations listed above. Some people will be getting the required nutrients from other foods and be well fed, some will reveal low intakes as the only sign of any problem, and others will have slight or severe biochemical abnormalities or severe clinical symptoms. In such a community, there will be some deaths from the deficiency disease. Deaths from nutritional deficiency are usually regarded as the tip of the iceberg: for every death there will be many cases of milder deficiencies.

The nutrition survey will pinpoint the problem and assess the degree of severity and the areas where the shortages are most severe, as well as the population groups at greatest risk. The final proof is delivered if, when the missing nutrient is added to the diet, either by a more nutritious food being introduced or by a common article of the diet being enriched, the disease is virtually wiped out.

AN EXPERIMENT IN DIET ENRICHMENT: RICE

In the Philippines experiment of 1948, rice was enriched with a nutrient that had been found to be deficient. At that time beri-beri was a common cause of death among children and adults. The disease affected 150 people in every 100 000 of the population, and deaths amounted to 24 000 in 1947. It was well recognized at that time that this was due to a diet relying very largely on polished white rice which was therefore low in vitamin B1. The peninsula of Bataan was selected for experiment, since it is geographically isolated and the food supply could be adequately controlled. Here 13 per cent of the population had beri-beri, and 164 people out of 98 000 died from this cause in 1947. The average daily intake of vitamin B1 was 0·7 mg, just about half the recommended level.

The rice sold in the experimental area was enriched with vitamin B1 and also with niacin and iron. Within only 3 months of the time this rice became available, there was a fall in mortality. After a year the death rate had fallen by 64 per cent, compared with a rise of 2 per cent in the control area where the rice was not enriched. After 21 months there were no deaths from beri-beri in the experimental area of Bataan, and the incidence of the disease had fallen by 89 per cent.

The actual process of enrichment posed difficult problems for the food technologists. First, it was physically impossible to enrich all the rice. Secondly, the colour and flavour of the food were not to be altered by the treatment. Thirdly, the added vitamin had to be stable over the usual period of storage. And fourthly, there was the problem of adding powdered nutrients to grains of rice. A technique had to be found whereby the powder would not settle out at the bottom of the packet or be rinsed off the food when the housewife washed the rice before cooking.

The first problem was overcome by preparing a pre-mix consisting of rice enriched at 200 times the required level and then diluting this with 199 parts of ordinary rice. By this means only 1 kg of rice in every 200 kg eaten was treated.

The second problem, of trying to avoid altering the colour, ruled out the addition of vitamin B2 to the rice, since this vitamin is bright orange. The original intention had been to add all three of the common B vitamins since there was a low level of all three in the diet, although vitamin B1 was in shortest supply. Trials showed that when rice was enriched with vitamin B2 the housewife noticed the yellowish grains and discarded them believing them to be bad. It is clearly of the greatest importance that enriched food should not look or taste in any way different from ordinary food.

The problem of enriching the grains with a powder which would not wash off was overcome by spraying a solution of the vitamins onto the rice, and coating it with a film of protein (zein). Thus the additives would not be lost when the housewife washed the rice, but would be released during digestion.

The interaction of social and economic factors with nutrition is well illustrated by the post-1950 history of this project in the Philippines. After so dramatic a demonstration of the life-saving effects of food enrichment, it would be expected that all the rice in the country would be enriched in the same way as all flour in Great Britain is enriched. However, a problem arose because some rice millers involved in the scheme discovered that the chemist could check their tax payments. If a vitamin preparation were provided to the rice millers and the enriched rice then analysed, it would be possible for the chemist to deduce the total amount of rice the millers were treating, and so arrive at the correct amount of tax they owed on the rice that they milled. To avoid this, the various milling interests blocked legislation aimed at compelling rice enrichment. The alternative has been to put enriched rice on the market and to encourage people to buy it. This is certainly not as successful a procedure as compulsory enrichment.

HUMAN EXPERIMENTS IN NUTRITION

One reason for the lack of precise information about human needs is that so small a number of subjects have taken part in experiments. The difficulties are very considerable. However, a series of human experiments were carried out in Sheffield between 1942 and 1944 from which valuable information of the requirements of human beings for vitamins A and C was obtained.

The subjects were 26 young men who had conscientious objection to joining the army but were willing to risk their health to make a contribution to human well-being. The first experiment on vitamin A requirements extended over 2 years, since well-fed people carry a large reserve of the vitamin in their livers. The subjects were provided with diets completely devoid of vitamin A or (in the nomenclature used at that time) its precursor, carotene.

The concentration of the vitamin in the blood did not begin to fall until the liver reserves were nearing depletion. The first sign of shortage was inability to see in dim light —night-blindness. The skin changes seen in people existing for many years on low levels of the vitamin were not seen in all the experimental subjects, so it is not clear whether or not this is a specific sign of vitamin A deficiency. When the subjects in the Sheffield experiment showed deficiency signs they were given various known amounts of vitamin A and the results were used to determine—actually to confirm—optimum requirements.

One difficulty in interpreting the results of human experiments of this kind is that the conditions are entirely different from normal human experience. People who normally live on diets low in any nutrient do so for periods of many years, and their diets are generally low in other nutrients, and possibly low in energy, also. Experimental subjects, on the other hand, are living under good environmental conditions on a good diet that is lacking only the one nutrient under investigation—and that nutrient is completely absent. One would never expect to see a 'pure' vitamin deficiency in a poorly-fed community; no-one is eating a good diet lacking only a single nutrient. So it is not surprising to find differences between the experimental subjects and those in whom the deficiency has been diagnosed 'in the natural state'.

The same volunteers carried out a vitamin C experiment in 1944. Since vitamin C is water-soluble with no specific organ storage in the body (in contrast to vitamin A), it was expected that the subjects would show signs of deficiency in a few weeks. Home Office permission was given for experiments in which the subjects were deprived of all vitamin C for a month. Nothing happened in that time. Permission was given to extend the period month by month, and it took as long as 5 months before signs began to appear in some subjects. There must therefore be enough vitamin C dispersed throughout the tissues of the body to last this long. The results also showed that the amount in the blood-plasma could fall to zero without any signs of scurvy; it was only after the levels in the white blood cells had fallen to zero that signs began to appear.

The final results of this experiment showed that scurvy could be cured or prevented with 10 mg of the vitamin per day. But vitamin C is also concerned in wound healing, and it was shown that wounds healed only slowly with this amount; 20 mg of vitamin C per day was needed to support normal rates of healing. To cover the possibly higher needs of the non-average person, the recommended intake was set at 30 mg per day.

OPTIMUM DIET AND GROWTH

Yet another aspect of the problem 'How much is needed?' is summed up by asking 'For what purpose?' Are we asking for a diet that will produce rapid growth, early maturity, long life, beauty, intelligence, freedom from infection, strength, or what? In general, the answer is that we want a diet that will promote a 'good' rate of growth, maintain health, and support a long and disease-free old age—all rather vague generalizations. Only growth-rate can be measured with any precision, but how fast should it be?

Certainly a poor diet restricts growth, and maximum growth rates require a good diet. Conversely, a slow growth rate or an obviously stunted child is indicative of a poor diet, and a rapid growth rate or a tall child is evidence that the diet has been adequate; but we do not know what rate of growth is optimum. Is the fastest growth best? Through the very nature of nutritional research we have tended to use growth rates as criteria of nutritional adequacy and therefore to regard the fastest growth as the best.

One of the main methods used in early investigations was to feed experimental animals a purified diet instead of natural foods. On such diets the animals lost weight and eventually died. When foods such as liver, yeast, cod-liver oil, or butter were added, the rats would maintain weight or grow. The experimenter would therefore conclude, quite correctly, that there was an essential nutrient in the added food. Chemical separation, aided at each stage by a test growth experiment, would finally isolate the nutrient. When the newly isolated nutrient was added to their diets the animals grew faster. It was as a result of this type of experiment that fast growth became the hallmark of good nutrition.

Without any question, a diet that is inadequate in almost any respect will result in poor growth and, conversely, an adequate diet will allow rapid growth, but there is no evidence to indicate that rapid growth is a 'good thing'. On the contrary, animal experiments have shown that a diet restricted enough to stunt growth, but not to cause ill-health, fosters longer life. This was first shown by McCay in 1935. He fed half a litter of rats on a normal, good diet, and they grew rapidly. The other half were given a diet restricted in amount but containing all the nutrients; they did not gain (or lose) weight but maintained themselves at less than half the weight of their big brothers. After about 2 years they were given the full diet and immediately began to gain weight, approaching, but not reaching, the weights of their big brothers. By this time the average life-span of rats had elapsed, and soon after this the well-fed rats died. But the previously underfed rats continued to live for about 6 months longer than their well-fed litter mates—6 months in a total of 30 months is a considerable increase (Fig. 3.4).

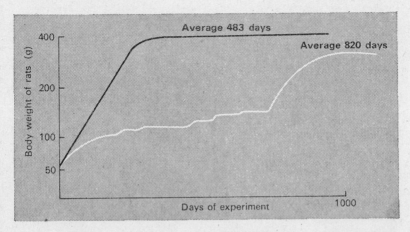

FIG. 3.4. McCay's experiment: a restricted food intake lengthened the life span of male rats (McCay, 1935. *J. Nutrit.*).

Since then this type of experiment has been repeated on many different species with similar results, although we do not know if this principle applies to man. In animal experiments we arrange for all conditions to be identical except the one single factor under investigation. Under practical conditions several factors operate at the same time.

There are many factors that influence energy utilization and growth in children. Dr. Widdowson of Cambridge observed the growth of children in two schools in Germany where, despite the same food intake, the children in one school grew faster than in the other. Deeper investigation revealed that the more rapid growth took place in the school where the children received greater care and affection; when the stricter and less affectionate staff from the second school were changed, the previously lower growth rate changed. Growth is also slowed when sleep is poor, probably because of reduced secretion of growth hormones. Another complicating factor is that babies born small tend to remain small.

The effect of improved nutrition on growth was clearly shown by observations of Japanese living in the United States. For many years it was believed that the Japanese were genetically smaller than Europeans. When some Japanese families emigrated to the United States, it was found that many of them grew considerably taller than the brothers and sisters that they had left behind—it was a question of nourishment rather than genetics. Even stronger evidence came to light when school meals in Japan were supplemented after 1945. During the next 10 years the average height of children in each group increased considerably, so that eventually a child of 12 years was 6 cm taller than a child of the same age had been 10 years earlier. It is not clear whether smallness is a drawback but the Japanese observations did show that diet had been limiting growth. More distinct evidence of the effect of diet comes from figures for the incidence of disease and death rates. The figures given earlier for the ill-health and deaths from beri-beri are a clear indication of a nutritional deficiency.

A more complex picture was provided by accident in Stockton-on-Tees in England between 1923 and 1932. The slum area of one part of the town was due for rebuilding in 1923, and 700 people from an area called Housewife Lane were moved into new, self-contained houses in Mount Pleasant. In the adjacent area of Riverside 1300 people stayed behind in slum houses. Each of the new houses had a bath, a kitchen range, a well-ventilated food store, and a wash-boiler—all one could expect in those days to make a family happy and healthy.

Before the removal, the death rate in both slum areas had been greater than the rest of the town; 23 per 1000 per year in Housewife Lane and 26 per 1000 per year in Riverside. When the figures were collected 5 years after rehousing, the expected fall in the death rate in the new houses had not come about. Instead, the death rate in Mount Pleasant had *risen* from 23 to 33 per 1000, while the rate in the old slum of Riverside showed a slight improvement to 23.

The explanation for the unexpected change in the death rate was found in the diets of the inhabitants of the two areas. Many of the families were unemployed and had only a small sum of money available for food. When they were moved into the new houses the rents were raised from the equivalent of 23p per week to 45p. Their old neighbours in Riverside were still able to spend 19p per week on food, while those in the new houses had only 14p available. The good effects of the improved housing and sanitation were overcome by the bad effects of a poorer diet.

HOW MUCH?

So we can now marshal the facts. (a) Nutrition is an important factor controlling growth, health, and freedom from disease, but there are other factors involved. (b) Under experimental conditions we can assess, within the limits of individual variation, the optimum quantities needed for various groups of the population. (c) Under practical conditions of life the figures are no longer precise and the multifarious stresses and strains affect the requirements. (d) Human beings adapt very well to shortages and surpluses, but whether this is beneficial or not we cannot tell. (e) When offered a variety of attractive foods, most people consume far more than they need for nutrients. Thus there is little or no fear of nutrient shortage, but surpluses and imbalance may introduce new problems. Perhaps all these variables explain, to some extent, why the nutritionist cannot be more precise about telling people what they should consume and finding out whether they are marginally deficient in some nutrient.

The large number of variables involved also explains why recommended intakes can vary from one authority to another, although the following factors are also involved. (a) There is often inadequate evidence so that the eventual figure becomes a matter of the opinion of the majority of the committee in question—a figure that can be changed by the next committee. (b) All tables clearly state that they are intended for a particular country (although the Food and Agriculture Organization Tables are intended for general use). For example, we may not benefit by eating a diet with more than 6 per cent protein, but people in Great Britain or the United States would not accept a diet with only 6 per cent protein, since they habitually eat a diet containing 10–12 per cent protein. It would be ill-advised for a national committee to recommend people to eat food that they do not like. (c) There may be good reasons for setting target figures for nutrients higher or lower than has been scientifically determined. It may be bad politics to set a target that is out of reach of most people in a poor country, and so the committee may set a temporary lower target. Alternatively, they may decide that people will strive to reach a higher target and may set it higher than in other countries. (d) The requirements for a nutrient may be affected by the other ingredients of the diet, so that figures for one community may be different from those of another which has a different basic diet.

4

What we eat

Food is the biggest industry in Britain with a turnover of £12 000 million per year. It is a sobering thought for fat and thin alike, that everyone eats about 35 tonnes of food in his lifetime—about half a tonne a year—so the size of the food industry is not so surprising.

NATIONAL TASTES

It is said that it is possible to tell a great deal about a person from his bookshelf; what can be deduced about a nation from its food habits? The British are often described as a nation of fish-and-chip eaters, specializing in soggy cabbage and roast beef, with regional preferences for Cornish pasties, Lancashire hotpot, and haggis. They are also great sweet-eaters, sucking and chewing their way through more than 600 000 tonnes a year (half chocolate and half sugar confectionary), which is more than 10 kg per head per year for every man, woman, and child.

Does it reflect any national differences when we find that the British eat two and a half times as much canned pineapple as the French, while the French eat two and a half times as much fresh pineapple as the British? What can be deduced about the British from their consumption of pickles—7000 tonnes of piccalilli, 15 000 tonnes of sweet pickles, and 22 000 tonnes of pickled onions a year?

Potatoes play a large and important part in the British diet: 'large', because 5 million tonnes are eaten annually, and 'important', because potatoes provide a quarter of the vitamin C and a tenth of the niacin and vitamin B1. Part of this large intake supports the potato chip industry, whose 14 000 retail shops have an annual turnover of £50 million and use half a million tonnes of potatoes. In addition, another quarter of a million tonnes of potatoes are sold as frozen chips.

However, the great English 'chip' is really the 'French fried' since it was introduced from France in 1880. John Rouse, an Oldham engineer, invented a mobile chip-making machine and gave away free chips with fish to popularize the sales of fish. The potato crisp industry is much newer; only small amounts were sold in the 1930s, and the sales increased rapidly only after 1950. The tonnage of potatoes used is not far short of that sold in chip shops, about 400 000 tonnes a year—mostly in 1-oz (28-g) packets. A total of £17 million-worth of potato crisps, puffs, sticks, and straws were sold in Great Britain in 1970. Some 47·5 per cent were flavoured with salt and vinegar, 13·7 per cent with cheese and onion, 7·9 per cent with bacon, 6·3 per cent with chicken, while 10·4 per cent had 'other flavours'.

The British are not generally renowned for their consumption of baked beans, but they eat $\frac{1}{3}$ million tonnes of beans-in-tomato-sauce every year.

Carbonated drinks, such as fizzy lemonade, have been with us for a long time, and a million litres are drunk in an average year—more if there is a hot summer. Fruit squashes and comminuted drinks (which include the whole crushed fruit) are newer developments. Since they are drunk after being diluted with water, they probably outstrip carbonated drinks with sales of 90 million litres of squash and 160 million litres of comminuted drinks.

Just behind Denmark, the British are the biggest eaters of quick-frozen foods in Europe, eating 10 kg (22·5 lb) per head per year. This is twice as much as is eaten in Germany and Holland, five times much as in France and ten times as much as in Italy. The figures are small, however, compared with the United States where the consumption of frozen foods is 35 kg (78 lb) per head.

Such detailed statistics are in marked contrast with some areas of the world where it is difficult to obtain any figures, let alone accurate ones, for such fundamental items as births, deaths, and ages of children. Perhaps rather than distinguishing between developed and developing countries, or rich and poor, when the question now often asked is 'which is which?', it may be clearer to distinguish between countries with and without detailed tabulations such as those listed above.

WHERE WE GET OUR NUTRIENTS

No one food contains all the nutrients that we need, so, quite apart from the question of monotony, we need to eat a variety of different types of food. Some foods, however, provide a large proportion of one or more of the nutrients that are needed, so they are of special importance in the diet. For example (Table 4.1), the average Briton obtains the greater part of his protein from only three sources— liquid milk (18 per cent), meat of various kinds (28 per cent), and bread (17 per cent). Cereals as a whole—flour, bread, rice, breakfast cereals, etc.—supply as much as 26 per cent of the average protein intake.

It is somewhat surprising that all the foods, including protein-rich foods like fish, eggs, peas, and beans, supply only a quarter of the protein. This is simply a reflection of the amount eaten—1200 g (40 oz) of bread and 1500 g (50 oz) of potatoes a week compared with 150 g (5 oz) of fish and 150 g (5 oz) of eggs.

The energy supply comes from a larger number of foods with milk, meat, and cereals providing between them 56 per cent of the total. Sugar and preserves account for 11 per cent of the average energy intake and if sugar used in manufactured foods is included, this figure rises to over 20 per cent. Fats supply 15 per cent of the energy, but this does not include the fat in foods like milk, kippers, and bacon, nor the fat used in the preparation of cakes, biscuits, and

TABLE 4.1

(a) Main sources of nutrients in the average British diet (1971)
(Percentage of total intake contributed by each food)

Food	Energy	Protein	Iron	Calcium	Vitamins					
					A	B1	B2	Niacin	C	D
Milk	11·4	19·0		49·5	13·4	14·5	36·5	12·8	0	
Cheese	2·3	5·0		10·8	4·4					
Meats	16·7	28·1	28·2		24·7	18·8	20·6	34·6		
Fish	1·0	4·3								18·7
Eggs	2·0	5·2	7·1		10·9		8·1			17·2
Butter	6·6	0			16·6					9·9
Margarine	3·9				9·0					35·8
Sugar and preserves	11·1		0							
Potatoes	4·6	4·0	7·9	0	0	11·1	0	9·1	26·2	0
Carrots			10		13·9					
Other vegetables		4·9			5·2	6·0		5·3	46·5	
Fruits									40·1	
Bread	14·3	16·8	17·9	14·3		23·3		11·1		

TABLE 4.1

(b) *Contribution to the average British diet (1971) by meat of various types as a percentage of total intake*

	Ounces† per week	Energy	Protein	Fat	Iron	Vitamins		
						B1	B2	Niacin
Beef and veal	8·0	3·0	6·8	5·0	9·2	0·9	3·5	9·5
Mutton and lamb	5·4	2·3	3·8	4·3	2·9	1·4	2·7	5·8
Pork	5·0	1·7	1·8	3·5	0·8	5·2	1·2	3·2
Bacon (uncooked)	5·1	3·2	2·8	6·8	1·5	4·8	1·6	2·0
Liver	0·8	0·2	0·8	0·2	3·3	0·6	5·5	2·6
Poultry (uncooked)	4·7	0·8	3·7	0·8	1·6	1·2	4·8	
Sausages	3·7	1·9	2·1	3·2	1·5		0·7	1·7
Other meat‡	8·2	3·6	6·5	5·7	7·6	5·5	4·3	7·0
TOTAL meat	39·0	16·7	28·1	29·8	28·2	18·8	20·6	36·6

National Food Survey 1973

‡*Other meat (ounces† per week)*

Offals other than liver	0·5	Other canned and cooked meat	2·5
Bacon, ham (cooked and canned)	0·9	Rabbit and game	0·1
Chicken (cooked)	0·2	Meat and sausage pies	0·7
Corned meat	0·4	Other meat products	2·8

† To convert to grams, multiply ounces by 28·4.

chocolates. If all sources of fat are taken into account, then they supply over 40 per cent of the average energy intake.

The amount of fat eaten has been increasing steadily over the years and is very much greater in the richer countries than in the poorer areas of the world. In Great Britain the consumption of 'visible fats' (butter, margarine, salad oils, and cooking fats) has risen from 107 g (3·5 oz) in 1955 to 119 g (4 oz) in 1971. In the United States fat consumption is 156 g (5·2 oz) and current trends in food manufacture and consumption suggest that this pattern will continue. This has lead, as discussed elsewhere, to the medical recommendation that fat intake should be reduced as a possible help to prevent heart disease. The relative amounts of butter and margarine eaten have, in the past, depended largely on price and social attitudes. However, the recent publicity given to heart disease and the fact that vegetable fats are relatively less harmful has modified this.

In the United States in 1950 the ratio of butter to margarine eaten was 11 : 6 (5 kg butter and 2·7 kg margarine per head per year); in 1970 the ratio was 5 : 11. In Great Britain, where butter is relatively cheap, the ratio is 5·5 : 3 in favour of butter. The toll taken by heart disease has not been so widely publicized in Great Britain, and social attitudes to margarine persist.

When we come to vitamins the main sources are few, although many foods contain small amounts. A quarter of the vitamin A intake comes from liver and another quarter from butter and margarine. One single food, carrots, supplies 14 per cent of the total vitamin A intake. This is an average figure for the whole population of Britain including carrot-abstainers as well as carrot-lovers, so it is likely that some individuals are obtaining the greater part of their vitamin A from this one food.

Some 40 per cent of the vitamin B1 is supplied by cereals, largely because it is added to all white flour; 20 per cent is supplied by meat; 14 per cent by milk; and 11 per cent by potatoes. The other two B vitamins come from fewer foods: 40 per cent of the vitamin B2 comes from milk and 20 per cent from meat, and 35 per cent of the niacin comes from meat and 27 per cent from cereals (it is added to white flour). Vitamin D is present in very few foods: 36 per cent comes from margarine, to which it is added by law, and 17 per cent from eggs.

The important minerals are also supplied by only a few foods: 50 per cent of the calcium comes from milk and 14 per cent from bread (calcium is added to flour). Small amounts of iron are found in many foods, but there are very few rich sources, and iron-deficiency anaemia is the commonest nutritional disorder in most of the Western world. Meat supplies 28 per cent of the average iron intake, and bread, to which iron is added by law, supplies 18 per cent. There are also a large number of mineral salts, such as magnesium, manganese, copper, zinc, etc., that are needed in small amounts, and these are found in a wide variety of foods.

We eat food, not nutrients, and the food must be attractively presented before we will eat it. So it is possible to have a food rich in nutrients but too unattractive to be eaten. It is also possible to have very attractive foods that are low in nutritional content. Indeed, one of the demands of the overweight person is for attractive foods that are low in calories.

The quality of food is therefore twofold: it must have both 'eating quality' and nutritional quality. Having 'eating quality' means it has an attractive appearance (eye-appeal), otherwise it may not even be tasted; it must appeal to the nose and the palate; and it must have an acceptable texture. It must, of course, be free from any harmful constituents, whether put there by nature or by man, and finally the diet as a whole, although not each individual food, must supply all the energy, protein, vitamins, and minerals needed for health.

One of our problems is that we have no instinctive ability to select nutritious foods. If we were offered smoked salmon, caviare, cream buns, and brandy, we might enjoy life but only for a short time—we would die from vitamin C deficiency. Many people in various parts of the world do suffer from nutritional deficiencies, although the foods that supply the missing materials are available. We have either to learn enough about food values to enable us to select the right foods, or to be supplied with complete foods, such as by enriching with the required nutrients, so that we cannot fail to consume all that we need. Generally speaking, when people can afford it, they tend to widen their choice of foods and having a greater variety gives them a good statistical chance of obtaining the whole range of nutrients. It is only when the diet bcomes restricted through poverty, lack of availability, or faddism that shortages are likely to occur.

Most people, of course, eat what they like, and even high prices are not always a deterrent. In Great Britain we spend nearly one-third of our total food bill on meat, and only 12 per cent on vegetables and 6 per cent on fruit (Table 4.2).

TABLE 4.2

Money spent on different foods in Great Britain in 1973

	Amount spent (£ millions)	Per cent of expenditure on food
Meat	2573	30·4
Dairy produce	1286	15·2
Bread and cereals	1007	11·9
Vegetables	978	11·6
Sugar, preserves, confectionary	727	8·6
Fruit	513	6·1
Beverages	467	5·5
Fish	334	3·9
Fats	313	3·7
Other manufactured foods	262	3·1
Total	8460	
Alcoholic drinks	3539	

Such figures are, of course, averages. Vegetarians spend nothing on meat, and many omnivores spend very much more than 6 per cent of their food bill on fruit just because they like fruit.

5

One man's meat

After learning what we need and how much we need for good health, it is fair to ask the nutritionist 'What is the perfect diet?' The answer is that there are many thousands of good diets, but no such thing as the perfect one. We can obtain the nutrients that we need from an extremely wide variety of foods, and people in different parts of the world are perfectly healthy on very different menus.

In Great Britain it is common to eat wheat, bread and butter, fish and chips, meat, cabbage, milk, apples, and oranges. In Ghana it is common to eat cassava, yam, plantain, maize, garden eggs, okra, and fish. People on either diet can be quite well fed so long as they have enough.

We tend to be so busy looking at our own plates that we often do not notice how much other people's choices differ from our own. In a survey of a group of English university students, three-quarters of those asked had never eaten black pudding, half had never eaten kidney, and a third had never eaten heart. Five per cent of the group had never eaten cheese or eggs. This is clearly not the same as disliking something after having tried it; these are people who have never tried the food. Black pudding may not come the way of many people, but surely liver and kidney do?

Certainly each of us tends to eat the foods that he is used to, and to regard other people's eating habits as strange. It is strange for Englishmen to think of snails and frogs' legs as food; it is strange for the European to read of people who eat mice, large game such as elephants, or a variety of insects including caterpillars. And those who do habitually eat caterpillars after first squeezing out the intestinal contents, washing them, and then cooking them in peanut butter, may think it extraordinary to cook caterpillars by flinging them into hot ashes to straighten them out and singe their hair. The Ifugao of the Philippines eat three species of dragon fly and locusts. These are boiled, dried, and powdered. They also relish red ants, water bugs, and beetles, as well as flying ants, which are usually fried in lard. In Tierra del Fuego the only vegetable is fungus. In Thailand people eat the coffee-boring moth and the giant water bug which is said to taste like Gorgonzola cheese. It is also said that a beetle larva cooked in coconut water has an inside rather like soufflé. Should such dishes appear somewhat abhorrent to the habitual consumer of fish and chips, consider the thoughts of the stranger when he learns that we habitually eat the secretion of the mammary gland of one species of animal mixed with the ovum of another—which, following the French, we call an omelette.

Some communities impose cultural restrictions on the foods eaten by certain groups of people. It is frowned upon in Great Britain to give tea, coffee, or alcohol to small babies, and it was once believed and recommended that meat should not be given to children younger than 7 years old since it was thought that they could not digest it (paediatric textbook, 1928). The Murngin of Australia permit only men who are fathers to eat porcupine, emu eggs, snake eggs, and crayfish—a rule that would not impose much hardship on European bachelors.

In the Middle East a meal without bread is impossible, since bread is the meal and everything else is simply an accompaniment. In similar fashion many people in Great Britain used to regard it as something of a sin to eat meat or fish without bread—these were foods that were too expensive or too good to eat alone.

Another cultural difference is the type of meal to suit the time of day. The English breakfast traditionally was bacon and eggs or porridge, now partly replaced by cereal and milk, or even nothing at all. Meat and potatoes would rarely be regarded as a food suitable for breakfast, but it is common in the United States to breakfast on ham and fried sausages and to mix bacon, pancake, and maple syrup. Australians, to English eyes, eat their dinner at breakfast time.

Cultural, traditional, and religious reasons for eating or refusing specific foods are not difficult to understand; it is more difficult to explain why people, sometimes universally and sometimes in one region only, develop strong preferences for certain foods. For example, no self-respecting North American will start the day without his orange juice, however difficult this may be to obtain when he goes abroad. Yet in Great Britain manufacturers have lost a great deal of money over the years trying to persuade the public to buy orange juice. It is even more interesting because this is not an inbred American tradition but developed in the 1930s as the result of a high-powered advertising campaign. So why do similar campaigns fail in Britain? There seems no logical reason why some nations and some individuals prefer tea to coffee, whisky to gin, or beer to wine—or why corn flakes sell in large quantities compared with wheat flakes, which are very similar but not quite the same.

SOCIAL NUTRITION

It is important for the nutritionist (and also for the food manufacturer) to know why people eat what they do, and as a corollary, how their habits can be changed (for the better). A whole host of factors operate in that area known as 'social nutrition'. People's food preferences depend on availability, price, family tradition, communal tradition, religion, prestige, pressure of advertising and/or knowledge, fashion, legal factors, developments in food technology, and possibly even their physiology.

Most of us tend to eat what we are used to eating, and if even the colour is unusual, it will put us off. The expectation that butter is yellow (it is almost white in countries that do not dye their butter) has been exploited by dairy interests who feared that they would lose sales to the margarine manufacturers. For many years it was illegal to colour margarine in some of the United States, and a capsule of dye was provided. Since white fat-spread is very off-putting, sales were kept down. Similar legislation continued in South Africa until October 1971, where it had also been very effective; when it became legal to add colour to margarine, butter sales fell by 20 per cent (between 1 October 1971 and 31 May 1972).

Sometimes eating habits change—the consumption of potato crisps and yogurt has increased enormously in Great Britain in a very few years, and breakfast cereals have also been quickly accepted; many rice-eaters in other parts of the world have changed to wheat. But sometimes even expensive advertising campaigns fail to change habits, and many new products have failed to sell. It depends on which factor is the strongest in causing or preventing change. At one time high-yield varieties of rice were successfully introduced into Nepal. However, the new rice was successful only from the point of view that the farmer obtained double yields. Unfortunately, the people of Nepal prefer the granular rice, whereas the new variety was of the sticky type. As a result the new rice fetched only half the price of the old rice, and farmers gave up the harvesting and taking to market of double loads of half value.

The same problem arose in Latin America. High-yield maize must, of course, be of the same flavour, and texture as the traditional variety; but it must also make tortillas of exactly the same kind. When the Latin-American farmer arrived home to find his tortillas burned, his wife explained that the new maize did not stick so well to the sides of the cooking pot but fell into the bottom where the tortillas got overheated. Thus the new maize was rejected.

So high yields, good profits, and foods that are so nutritious that they will help to lengthen life are all factors that may be less important than taste or convenience when it comes to the crunch.

THE AVAILABILITY OF FOOD

Clearly, the most important factor in establishing the type
of food that we eat must be its availability. Climate will
decide whether we grow wheat, rice, or rye; river or lakeside
dwellers are more likely to eat fish than inland communities;
roads, mountains, and transport will control whether we
are restricted to locally grown foods.

It is probably difficult for anyone living in Great Britain,
where half the total food is imported, to think of depending
largely on what is grown locally. A food-importing country
can bring food from almost anywhere in the world (so long
as it has something to sell in exchange), and when foods are
out of season in one country they are imported from another,
so that in Great Britain oranges and apples, for example,
are available at all times. On the other hand countries that
grow their own supplies are reluctant to import products
that might be competitive and so have seasons when some
foods are not available.

Price must also be a factor controlling what we eat,
although this depends a great deal on what percentage of a
family's income may be devoted to food. In Great Britain
we spend, on average, only about a quarter of the family
income on food, which enables us to afford luxury foods
(Fig. 5.1). In the nineteenth century we in Great Britain
spent about 60 per cent of our income on food, and we had
little choice; this position still holds today in many countries.
The changing values of food are illustrated by the statement in the indentures of apprentices in Great Britain in
the nineteenth century that fresh salmon must not be served
more than three times a week—because it was such a cheap,
common food!

Although the price controls what we eat, the value of
food in monetary terms is a very relative matter. The consumer of caviare at £2 for 25 g is not deterred when the
price is doubled, but when the 15p loaf is increased in price
by 1p there is an outcry.

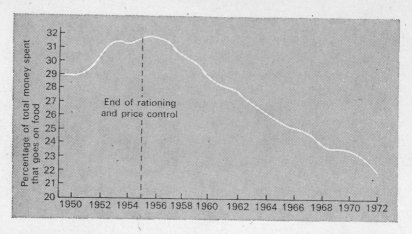

FIG. 5.1. The average expenditure on food in Great Britain (as a percentage of the total money spent).

HOW FAMILY TRADITIONS INFLUENCE DIET

If economics can affect food preferences in two different ways, so can mother's cooking. Generally our eating patterns are established in childhood, and we continue to eat such foods throughout life for a variety of reasons, including, so the psychologists tell us, the feeling of security that well-known foods give us. On the other hand, many a child has been put off cabbage for life either because his mother made him eat it or because she cooked it badly.

Investigations into the eating habits of immigrants into Great Britain showed that they ate English foods when they first arrived, and began to buy their traditional foods only after they had been in Britain for some years. The explanation of this unexpected behaviour was simply that traditional foods were expensive compared with English foods, and the poorly paid immigrant could not afford them. When he had been here for a few years and was earning more, he could afford his traditional foods. In general, even when people become largely assimilated into an alien community and adopt new forms of diet, some vestiges of their old eating habits tend to remain, even if only at weekends or festivals. Traditional dishes may continue to be eaten for generations, long after other ties have been broken. Thus bound up with family tradition is the tradition of the community, both in the positive sense of eating particular foods or in the negative sense of taboos.

TABOOS

Taboos arise for a variety of reasons. The soldiers of Madagascar were forbidden to eat hedgehog—it is an animal that retreats backwards when approached and might confer cowardice on those who consume it. The Kusasi in northern Ghana will not eat pawpaw (although there is a vitamin A deficiency in that area) because it is believed that the one who planted the tree will die. The Adangbes forbid children to eat eggs and meat for fear that they will then be unable to talk. The Ewes will not eat a certain type of fish because it has the same name as their clan and they would be eating their own souls.

Of two tribes (the Ashanti and the Kwahu) that live on the Pra river in Ghana, only one eats fish. The reason is that, 300 years ago, the River Goddess asked them what they most wanted. The Ashanti said food, and they take fish from the river; the Kwahu said money, and they are afraid to take fish from the river for fear of offending the Goddess.

The avoidance rule of the Shona tribe of Rhodesia show how well codified such beliefs can be. 'Do not eat what you have brought as a present for someone you are visiting, you may go bald'; 'do not eat the eggs or flesh of the nightjar, you might become habitually sleepy during the day'; 'do not eat groundnuts dug up by a cow and buried again, you may become absent-minded'.

Prejudices, taboos, and unfounded beliefs are not the prerogative of primitive peoples. In Great Britain and the United States there are people who believe firmly in the magical properties of honey, or pollen, or food grown in animal manure. People even in the most 'civilized society' will buy pills, potions, and copper bracelets because the witch doctor—disguised as a health-food specialist or television advertiser—tells them to do so.

Anyone who feels immune from such irrational beliefs should try eating dog or horse meat, or drinking his friend's blood. After all, as Dr. Magnus Pyke has pointed out, we willingly take our friend's blood into our veins (it is then called a blood transfusion).

Religious edicts can prevent people eating particular foods, such as pork, meat, fish, or even all animal foods, and, in the extreme, from eating vegetable foods that grow below ground. Religious rulings also prevent some people from eating at all on various fast days.

PRESTIGE FOODS

One of the wonders of the modern food world is the widespread consumption of Coca-Cola and Pepsi-Cola. In almost every country, rich or poor, city and countryside, this sweet brown liquor is drunk. One of the more feasible reasons why people buy it is that it is a relatively expensive imported product of American origin and therefore has a certain prestige value. The belief that certain foods are 'poor man's food' can prevent people eating them. For example it is just as bad to be seen eating radish in Nepal as to be seen driving last year's car in New York.

Margarine is a good example of how supposed social prestige can influence food consumption. Margarine has long been regarded as a substitute for butter. It was originally designed as a cheap substitute, but in recent years (certainly in Great Britain) some brands are more expensive than butter. Although margarine is widely eaten, such a practice was often regarded as being socially degrading— margarine was for the servants. Many housewives, even today, when asked if they buy margarine, confess to doing so, but hasten to add 'only for cooking, of course'. The manufacturers' advertisements have attempted to overcome British prejudice by telling television viewers that rich Americans, even when they own two cars and a yacht, buy margarine—what better example could there be? In the

United States, however, the 'health' aspect of a food sometimes outweighs the influence of prestige. This is indicated
by the fact that, since the general acceptance of the finding
that butter elevates the blood cholesterol and specially
prepared margarines do the reverse, margarine sales have
far outstripped butter sales in the United States.

ADVERTISING AND NUTRITIONAL INFORMATION

The layman may believe that advertising can achieve anything. The manufacturer knows that all the advertising
that he can afford will not change anyone's buying habits
unless his product is attractive and the price is right. But
all other things being equal, advertising will bring goods
to the attention of the potential buyer and will often persuade him to buy. It may also help to create prejudices and
beliefs, valid or otherwise.

Advertising can affect our eating habits; we are not sure
how far a knowledge of nutrition may do so. People generally
buy food because they like it, not because it does them
good. The United States has introduced legislation for
labelling foods with nutritional information, but there is
little evidence that anyone takes much notice. There is no
evidence to suggest that even nutritionists themselves mod-
ify their eating habits in the light of their scientific
knowledge.

Surveys among members of the general public have shown
little specific knowledge of nutrition, but a reasonable
innate knowledge of what is good for them. They are not
very concerned about nutrition, and many people (25 per
cent of those questioned in one survey) think that food has
little or no effect on health.

The varying extent of public knowledge is indicated by
one large survey carried out in 1969. This survey found that,
while a majority of those asked (75 per cent) not only
knew that milk was a source of protein, calcium, and
vitamins (and even knew what the calcium was useful for),
very few (less than 0·5 per cent) knew that vitamins were
added to margarine or that vitamins and minerals were

added to bread. This may have been due to two factors: first, milk advertising (with an emphasis on nutritive value) is carried out by a body called the National Dairy Council, an organization which sounds non-commercial and authoritative and therefore, presumably, believable. Secondly, milk is regarded by the general public as a natural food and therefore 'good', while bread and margarine are 'processed' foods and therefore not expected to be particularly nutritious.

FASHIONS IN FOOD

Foods, like clothes but perhaps not so distinctly, follow fashions. Popular personalities are used in order to set trends in eating just as they set trends in dressing. So we have periods where it is fashionable to be slim or even skinny, where kippers are lower class, where coffee is more middle class than tea, and so on. Advertisers make use of the stars of the day, footballers, TV personalities, or singers, to sell their foods.

Health-food addicts appear to be ever more easily swayed. This group certainly passes through phases of fashion-following, often as dictated by the latest book on the subject. Thus we see fads like cider-vinegar, pollen, vitamin E, bees' royal jelly, buckwheat or that naturally processed food, honey. We shall return to health-foods again in Chapter 6.

THE COMMON MARKET AND EUROPEAN EATING HABITS

In recent years the Common Market has had an effect, or has attempted to have an effect, on the composition and types of food eaten by the Community. The Market attempts to remove barriers to trade that extend along national boundaries and therefore committees have had to spend much time in standardizing foods.

The British like their sausages, white bread, and marmalade, but these products differ in composition from those eaten on the Continent. Europe is divided into nations that have cream in their ice-cream (such as France, Germany, Denmark, and Luxembourg) and others (including Britain, Holland, and Belgium) that make it from vegetable fats. In Britain 2 per cent salt is added to butter; on the Continent it is mostly unsalted. Since it is the farmers rather than the manufacturers that dominate the scene in France and Germany, they would like to see the salt omitted, because that would slightly increase the sales of butter.

As negotiations proceed over long periods of time and terminate with a veto by any nation that will not change its foods, it is becoming increasingly obvious that people cannot be easily persuaded to change their eating habits either by logical argument or in the interests of compromise.

FOOD TECHNOLOGY

Changes in the methods of production and processing of food are having an ever-increasing effect on eating patterns. The dietary changes produced by modern technology can be seen in every meal from breakfast to dinner.

The development of the broiler chicken has changed chicken from a luxury to a commonplace food. The invention of instant coffee has overcome (partially, at least) the British reliance on tea. The introduction of instant breakfast cereals changed our early-morning eating habits. The advent of frozen foods and the more recent introduction of home freezers have brought about changes, particularly in making 'out of season' foods available. Sales of wet fish were steadily falling earlier this century because the housewife considered the cooking of fish a messy business; the introduction of fish fingers stopped the decline and made fish much more popular. Technology has also made more unusual foods readily available, and the introduction of 'new' foods like scampi, avocado pears, and aubergines has contributed to our changing eating habits.

Such changes are bound to arise in a society where there is relative affluence. People are less and less dependent on their traditional staple foods, and they eat a wider variety of foods. The continuous fall in the consumption of our staple food, bread, over the past hundred years is a clear indication of this phenomenon in action.

'OLD FAVOURITES'

The potato

There are foods that retain their hold, whatever the changes, and the potato is one of these. The potato was first introduced into Europe 400 years ago but was not at first accepted. It gained acceptance in France when it was deliberately grown in a fenced plot labelled 'The King's Potatoes'. People were so curious and anxious to steal these potatoes that they became popular.

The potato was well established as an important part of the diet in Great Britain by the eighteenth and nineteenth centuries, with an intake averaging 1·5 kg per head per week. As recently as 1971 the average consumption was still 1·4 kg per head per week. Potatoes occupy a special place in nutrition in Great Britain since they supply a quarter of the average vitamin C intake, as well as being an important source of vitamin B1 and niacin, and they even supply 4 per cent of the protein consumed. However, this is not why people eat them. The question is, what would people eat instead of potatoes, alongside their meat and vegetables, or with their fish?

Potatoes are popular despite relative affluence because they are well known as a food, easy to prepare, and filling (which also means fattening to most people). Because they are cheap they are not associated with self-indulgence, but they are not looked down on as 'poor man's food', and are served even in expensive restaurants. They have a bland, neutral taste and can be prepared in many ways and eaten with a variety of other foods; indeed they help by diluting the strong and expensive taste of meat eaten at the same time. Psychologists tell us that we associate with eating potatoes a feeling of security and stability. Clearly, social nutrition is an intricate business.

The sausage

A food that has woven its way into the culture of Europe
is the sausage, a term which means different things to each
of the different nations of Europe. The sausage holds a
special place in British food history, apart from having
once been pronounced upon by the Lord Chancellor himself, being eaten to the extent of 5000 million sausages
(300 000 tonnes) a year, costing a total of £100 million.
Even at this level the British are overtaken by the greater
sausage-eaters of Germany.

The invention of this forerunner of convenience foods
is not known, but 2500 years ago there was already in
existence an ancient Greek play called *The sausage (Oraya)*.
Homer, wrote of 'the sausage, full of fat and blood'. Certainly the dried sausage, the salsus, was eaten in ancient
Rome.

There are said to be thousands of different recipes for
sausages; 800 varieties of sausage were exhibited at Berne
in Switzerland in 1907. The national and regional variations on the sausage theme within Europe are very great.
The British 'banger' differs considerably from the French
dried variety; it is, in fact, unique to Great Britain, and has
caused much discussion within the Common Market re-
garding its standardization as a food product. Even within
Great Britain there are regional differences: more sausages
are eaten in Scotland than in England; thin ones are preferred in the South and thick ones in the North; black
pudding is far more popular in the North than in the
South; beef sausages score over pork in the North and in
Scotland, while the reverse is true in the South.

Puffer fish and other strange addictions

If people like their own local foods and stick to them
throughout centuries of social change, people who risk real
harm rather than give up their favourites must be even
more addicted.

The puffer fish, *Tetra odontoidea*, is very much liked in

China and Japan. In most seasons of the year it is extremely poisonous, and there are frequent reports of deaths from eating this fish. The problem is recognized officially in Japan to such an extent that cooks must hold a special licence before being permitted to prepare the fish; they must be skilled in removing the toxic parts completely. Despite the risk clearly involved, people persist in eating the fish.

Almost parallel is the durian (*Durio zibethinus*) a fruit of south-east Asia, the consumption of which has been described (by an Englishman) as like eating sweet custard on the lavatory. It has a powerful and revolting odour that fills the streets when the fruit stall has durian in season and has led to a ban on bringing it into hotels in Malaysia. Those who like the flavour tell one to persist until the taste is acquired, but it might well be asked how man ever came to taste a food that has so powerful a means of putting him off.

From all this we can only conclude that when it comes to choosing a diet, man will usually do very much as he pleases (even if subconsciously he is influenced by the forces of tradition and advertising). Nutritionists have therefore been forced to include a study of man himself as part of their science.

6

Nature knows best—or does she?

We start the day with a glass of pasteurized, or chemically preserved, or canned orange juice, followed by a puffed, roasted, toasted, or exploded breakfast cereal on which we put pasteurized milk and brown or white granulated sugar. This is followed by any one of a variety of breads— white, brown or medium, rye or wheat—spread with butter or margarine and marmalade, and we wash all this down with an extract of tea or coffee.

About the only food that we may have eaten that had not passed through the hands of the manufacturers was orange juice freshly squeezed from a whole orange, but even that probably crossed the world in a gas-filled container or wrapped in paper impregnated with anti-mould agent. Of course, if we had eaten eggs and bacon, the eggs could have been fresh and unprocessed whether from free-range, deep-litter or battery hens, but that is about the limit of our consumption of unprocessed food at breakfast-time.

It is calculated that about 98 per cent of our food (on a calorie basis) is processed. This figure is high because most of the fresh foods, like fruits and vegetables, provide few calories. Why is this? Why is it considered necessary to process all these foods? Why can we not have fresh, crisp, tasty, nutritious foods without all this processing, without all the chemicals and colours and flavours added? There are two answers. We could not get enough fresh food, and we like processed foods.

Our crowded cities are supplied with foods from all over the world—orange juice from Florida, breakfast cereal from the maize of North America or Central Europe, sugar from the Carribean, bread from hard Canadian wheat, butter from New Zealand, marmalade from Seville oranges, and coffee and tea from any of a score of countries; even home-produced milk may come from the countryside 200 km away. To travel so far the food must be preserved—frozen, dried, canned, pickled, or treated chemically. It must last long enough to withstand the journey, stand on the shelf in warehouse and shop until we buy it, and still keep in the larder until we want to eat it.

PRESERVATION OF FOOD

The reasons for preserving foods are obvious, and the process is essential. We simply could not feed ourselves on fresh foods alone; only small communities living where the food is grown can do so. In earlier generations, and still today in some parts of the world, many people went hungry between harvests. This does not happen today where people have the money and the technical resources to store food between harvests. Fish and meat can be transported thousands of kilometres from areas where they are plentiful to areas where they are wanted; tropical fruits and vegetables can be made available all the year round.

Preservation is necessary because foods that are useful to man are equally useful to the bacteria, moulds, yeasts, and fungi that share our environment. Foods left for any length of time go 'bad': they grow mouldy or ferment or putrefy. Not only may they become unpleasant to taste and smell but they can also be harmful, since some of the types of bacteria (pathogens) that grow can cause disease. So food must be preserved not only to avoid waste but also to prevent disease.

The micro-organisms need warmth and moisture to grow. If the temperature falls, the growth slows down; if it falls low enough, the growth stops. If moisture is removed, they also stop growing. So foods go bad quickly in the warmth, will keep longer if kept cool, will keep longer still if chilled to the temperature of a refrigerator (around 0 °C), and will keep for many months if cooled right down to the temperature of the domestic freezer (−18°C). They will keep indefinitely when dried and kept dry.

Probably the most certain method of preserving food is to destroy all the organisms completely, usually by heat, although chemicals and ionizing irradiation are also effective in doing this. After it has been sterilized, the food must be protected from further contamination; this is the basis of bottling and canning.

Canning

Canning was first carried out on a commercial scale in England in 1832, and two of the earliest cans, one of mutton and one of veal, were opened in 1960. The mutton was then 110 years old and the veal 136 years. They were still sterile, although the structure of the meat and the fat had largely broken down so that the food could not be considered palatable.

While sterilization may be the surest method of preserving food, the rather high temperatures needed can spoil the colour, flavour, appearance, and nutritive value of the treated food. Pasteurization is a process in which the food is heated to a temperature sufficient to destroy the harmful bacteria (the pathogens), but not all the bacteria. The food is safe but not sterile, so it will not keep for more than a few days. The advantage is that at this lower temperature the food suffers less damage.

Enzyme action and quick freezing

Food also deteriorates through the action of its own enzymes; this happens when fruits and vegetables go bad. If you take a bite out of an apple and then leave it on the table, the exposed area quickly goes brown as a result of oxidation by the air, assisted by the enzymes in the fruit. Enzymes are also active in game, like pheasant or partridge, that is hung for several days before it is eaten, although in this instance the 'off' flavour is thought to be desirable.

Enzyme action can still continue, although more slowly, in a freezer at −18°C, so fruits and vegetables intended to be quick-frozen are first cooked briefly (that is, blanched) to destroy the enzymes. It is at this stage that there is some loss of nutritive value, when part of the water-soluble vitamins and minerals are washed into the cooking water, the amount depending on the food and how finely it has been cut up. After this stage of the process, frozen foods can be kept for months with no further change in flavour, texture, colour, or nutritional value.

Of all the methods of preservation, quick-freezing causes the least loss of nutritive value. If the cook remembers that the short cooking before freezing reduces the time needed for final cooking, there is not a great deal of difference between the nutritive value of fresh foods cooked and served immediately and cooked frozen foods. Fresh vegetables lose about half their vitamin C when cooked under the best conditions, while similar vegetables that have been blanched, frozen, stored six months, and then cooked (for a shorter time) lose about 60 per cent of their vitamin C. Much greater losses of vitamin C take place if food is kept hot and exposed to air instead of being eaten immediately. Mashed potato, for example, for which the air can get to the vitamin, can lose half its vitamin C if kept hot for 20 minutes; so if kept hot for an hour before being eaten only half of a half of a half (or 12½ per cent) of the original amount of vitamin C is left. Losses of other vitamins and nutrients are very much smaller than losses of vitamin C.

Drying and freeze-drying

Another way of preventing the growth of micro-organisms is to remove the water from the food. In earlier days, and still today in some parts of the world, the food was dried in the open air in the wind. This is a slow process. Depending on the weather, it often takes several days, during which all the vitamin C and a large part of the vitamins A and B1 are destroyed. Some foods, like fish and meat, do not lose much nutritive value in this way, but their flavour and texture are spoiled.

Modern factories dry foods under controlled conditions with less damage to the food, although considerable changes in eating quality and nutritional content do take place. A variety of drying equipment is used for different products: ovens (operating either in a vacuum or at atmospheric pressure), moving belts passing continuously through air heated to any required temperature, fluidized beds where pieces of food bounce along on jets of hot air, spray dryers, tower dryers, and freeze-dryers.

For freeze-drying the food is first frozen and then placed in a chamber under high vacuum, when the ice evaporates off without melting. This is the method of drying that does the least damage to the food. The finished food is dry, not frozen; it is frozen only during the process.

Jam

Another method of effectively removing water is to add a large quantity of sugar to hold the water so that it is not available to the bacteria or yeasts—this is the principle of making jam.

Pickling and salting

Chemicals can also be used to stop organisms from growing in foods. Sulpher dioxide or benzoic acid is now often added to fruit juices but salt and vinegar have been used for this purpose for hundreds of years. When food is preserved by pickling, the fermentation produces enough acid to prevent the growth of unwanted organisms.

Traditional processing

In principle, none of the above processes is new. Man has

dried, salted, pickled, and smoked his foods for thousands of years. Even cooling was used by the ancient Romans, who collected blocks of ice from frozen lakes in winter and kept them in caves to cool food in the summer. It is the techniques and the understanding of the scientific bases rather than the principles that have changed. Possibly only pasteurization, just over 100 years old, and the very modern processing by gamma-rays and X-rays can be considered 'new' methods.

The safety of preserving by adding chemicals will be discussed later. This method of preserving may be dubiously regarded by the general public, but we should recognize that new methods are often suspect, whereas traditional methods are generally accepted as being safe—despite any indication to the contrary. For example, the smoking of foods (a traditional method) preserves them for a short time because the outer surface is dried out, and at the same time chemical preservatives from the smoke are deposited on the food. Despite this, smoked foods have only a short life; they are not sterile. Smoke contains a range of chemical substances that have not been examined for safety, but because the process is so old it is accepted with little question. It is probably true to say that if smoking were introduced as a new process today, it would not be allowed.

TICKLING THE PALATE

A major reason for processing food is to make it more attractive and to add variety. Apart from being desired by the gourmet and the food seller, variety is important to the nutritionist because it helps to ensure an adequate intake of the whole range of nutrients. When the diet is restricted to a small number of food items, there can be a limitation of nutrient intake. Also a monotonous diet might be eaten in inadequate amount, through sheer boredom.

In some instances the process of preservation alters the food so much that it becomes virtually another product, with different texture and flavour, which may well be more popular than the original product. For example, canned salmon and canned pineapple are often preferred to the fresh products; fruit preserved as jam, and herrings pickled in vinegar, are quite different from their fresh forms; and instant coffee has taken its place among the other major hot beverages of mankind—tea, cocoa, and bean coffee.

Food colouring

While preserving food is essential, and variety in the diet is desirable, it may be questioned whether adding or restoring colour falls into either category. And yet food manufacturers frequently add colour, because otherwise the consumers will not buy. Colours are also added to foods to standardize them. The colour of fruit juices, for example, may vary with variety and season, but the consumer demands constancy of his food appearance at all times. Moreover, a pale orange juice looks as if it has been watered down.

At a time when some individuals were complaining about the 'unnecessary' addition of colours to foods, one of the largest British retailers tried the experiment of *not* colouring his canned green peas. During the sterilization process the garden pea loses much of its natural colour and becomes pale and rather unappetizing, so for many years manufacturers have added a green dye, solely to improve the appearance. Despite the retailer's advertisements of his dye-free product the project was a failure: people prefer their green peas to be green, even if it means the addition of artificial colours.

The point is that we like to find the expected colours in our foods, and are put off by unusual colours or lack of colour. Experiments with green custard and purple buns prove how much colour affects our food intake. It is for reasons like these that manufacturers add a red dye to raspberry-flavoured jelly, and add yellow dye to cornflour to make it into 'custard' powder, and dye improperly smoked kippers.

Texture

Chemical aids are also used to improve texture. New potatoes have become sufficiently popular for manufacturers to can them during the season for consumption all the year round; the texture softens during the process, but it can be restored by the addition of calcium salts. Meat is juicier when phosphates are injected into the tissue; cakes maintain their stickiness with 'humectants'; mayonnaise and sauces are chemically emulsified. The list is endless, and this subject will be mentioned again when we discuss chemical additives in general.

'IMPROVING' FOOD

The manufacturer can tickle our palates, and our other senses, but he can also make life a little easier for us. Take, for example, ordinary table salt that pours freely from the salt cellar. Before manufacturers started to add carbonate as an anti-caking agent, it was a nuisance to have to bang the salt cellar on the table top or prick out the clogged holes with the prongs of a fork. It was even worse when we had to grate the large blocks of solid salt that our grandmothers were faced with.

Perhaps a more marked improvement, even if unknown to the younger housewife, is the addition of an anti-spattering agent to some frying oils. Our mothers had burns from splashes of hot oil almost every time they fried fish or chips. Drops of water from the food suddenly turned into steam at the temperature of the hot oil, and, since one drop of water expands 1700 times when it is turned into steam, each produced an explosion—with drops of boiling oil as shrapnel. The improvement was obtained by adding a derivative of lecithin which prevents the drops from coalescing, so that they boil off without exploding. Today only the very careless housewife gets oil burns, and non-spattering oil is taken for granted.

Convenience foods

A convenience food is defined as a food on which the manufacturer has carried out a large part of the preparation, so saving the time and trouble of the consumer. While the most obvious examples of a convenience food are instant coffee, soup mixes, and instant puddings, there were many other examples long before these. Ready-baked bread is a convenience, canned beans are ready to eat—indeed, all bottled and canned foods have already been cooked and are a convenience.

Convenience foods provide a neat example of how affluence and food technology advance together. Only when spare money is available can the consumer afford to pay the manufacturer to do some of his work for him. Otherwise he buys the raw materials and prepares the food himself. Generally, of course, the technology and the affluence stimulate one another, so that the manufacturer is able to offer new food experiences to eager customers. New tastes, new colours, new shapes, and new forms of presentation are by no means essential, so that processing for these reasons is not necessary, but to most people they are desirable features of life. Presumably those new ventures that are not desirable or attractive are the ones that fail their marketing tests.

Packaging

Side by side with modern food processing has been the development of packaging. This has led to greater care being taken of our food and vastly improved standards of hygiene. Not so many years ago the grocer had a barrel of herrings on a sawdust floor by the side of a sack of sugar and another of dried peas. On the counter was a huge slab of butter and a side of bacon. These were exposed to the dust of the streets, the germs of passers-by, and the probing fingers of the careful housewife, not to mention the dirty hands, hair, and general contamination of the shopkeeper and his staff. The bacon was sliced on a machine that would serve as a useful store-cupboard for a class of microbiologists, the herrings were picked out of the barrel with the shop-keeper's fingers, and it was not unknown for the sacks of food to be 'labelled' by the dogs of waiting customers.

Factory production, supermarkets, and packaging have swept most of this sort of thing away from industrialized communities, although such conditions certainly persist in many underdeveloped communities. In the West the sugar is now automatically packed into fixed-size packets—it is much easier for the Weights and Measures Inspector to control them than thousands of shopkeepers. The bacon is sliced and packed in hygienic plastic film under controlled factory conditions, and the pickled herrings come in sealed jars. All this is just as well, since most human beings have not improved their habits of hygiene in step with other advances.

This is far from being a matter of aesthetics alone (although packaging can make food much more attractive to the customer); it is a matter of improving health and controlling disease. Large churns of raw milk, carrying tubercle bacilli and other pathogens, have given way to sealed bottles of pasteurized or sterilized milk, and food-handling has been markedly reduced, if not eliminated, in automated food factories. The newly developed sciences of microbiology, nutrition, and food have been put to good use in scientifically controlled large production units. Sometimes the price we have to pay for all this automation and packaging is some loss of flavour, texture, and nutritional value, and part of the good processing of food includes attempts to restore these qualities.

CHEMICAL ADDITIVES IN FOOD

Several thousands of chemical substances are currently added to foods during manufacture for the purposes already described. They act as preservatives, as fat antioxidants, to restore the colours and flavours impaired during the process, to assist the retention of texture, to slow down the rate at which baked goods get stale, to emulsify mixtures such as

mayonnaise, to keep cakes soft and sticky, to control acidity
or alkalinity, to restrain metallic ions from discolouring
foods, and much more.

The addition of chemical substances has given rise to a
great deal of controversy, much of it ill-informed. The word
'chemical' raises protests and feelings of horror, but a
chemist could point out that *all* food constituents—fats,
carbohydrates, vitamins, and so forth—are chemicals. In
fact our bodies and our world are made entirely out of
chemicals. The issue is whether or not the chemicals that
we *add* to our food (termed 'chemical additives' or 'processing aids') are in any way harmful. To find that they
are harmful and to ban them is usually easy; what is much
more difficult is to prove that they are harm*less*. It is impossible to prove this sort of negative attribute, and all we
can hope to do is to establish a reasonable degree of safety.

Chemical additives are used in food in very small
amounts, about 0·1–0·01 per cent of the food (one part in
a thousand or ten thousand), but we must remember that
we continue to eat such foods for a lifetime, and the effect
may be cumulative. However, there is no evidence, at least
in Great Britain, that anyone has ever suffered any harm
from an intentional food additive (as distinct from
accidental contamination with poisons, pesticide residues,
or bacteria)—but neither is there any proof to the contrary.

As explained below the evidence is difficult to examine,
and absolute conclusions are impossible, but it is comforting
to note that, despite the rapid multiplication of the use
of chemical additives in recent years, people live longer
than ever before—so they cannot be all that bad for us.
On the other hand, we do not know whether any of the
common, everyday ills are not aggravated or even caused by
any of these substances, and the industrialized communities
of the Western world do now suffer 'diseases of affluence'.
Thus the effect on humans of chemical food additives continues to be a topic of hot debate.

Safety-testing

All new chemical additives are tested extensively before
they are put on the market. The best way we can do this
is to try them out on animals. Possibly the most difficult
question to answer is how big a dose should be fed to the
test animal, bearing in mind that almost every food, natural
as well as processed, is harmful if given in large enough
amounts. If one-quarter of the diet fed to a rat is vitamin
C, the rat will die in 3 weeks; does that mean that we
should not consume vitamin C? Babies have died after
being given salt in their bottles by mistake for sugar; does
this mean that we must never eat salt? Large volumes of
water, of the order of 3 or 4 litres, drunk in a short time
causes immediate death by diluting the salts in the blood
reaching the brain; does this mean water is harmful?

Colours, flavours, preservatives, and other substances are
used at levels of 0·01–0·1 per cent in food, and such small
amounts can be fed to animals for a lifetime with no
observable effects. So we have the problem of deciding how
large the test dose should be in order to establish a margin
of safety.

Another problem lies in the choice of test animal to
serve as an index for man. Substances shown to be harmful
to one species have been found harmless to another because
the body deals with them in a different way—they follow
a different metabolic pathway. So a substance found to be
safe in the test animal may not be safe for man, and vice
versa.

Then what do we look for in the test animals? Certainly
obvious ill-health or the slowing down of growth would rule
out the use of a substance in human foods without proceeding to any further tests. However, even growth may
not be a clear criterion, since the flavour of the test substance at high dose levels may reduce the amount of food
eaten and so slow the growth for that reason. We might
say that any change caused by the added substance must
be regarded as being potentially harmful and as indicating
that it should be ruled out, but changes can be caused by

simple alterations in eating habits, that is, eating the same foods as usual but at different times of the day. For example, if anyone eats his ordinary food in five small meals instead of three larger meals, he will lay down less fat and more protein in the body and alter the level of various hormones. When such changes can be caused just by the pattern of eating, it is difficult to decide what changes should be regarded as harmful.

There are no satisfactory answers to these questions, but schemes of testing have been drawn up with international approval which provide a reasonable degree of certainty that an additive is safe. They can, however, give no final proof. After all the tests have been carried out, it is still necessary to judge each set of results against the background of the possible use of the substance, and, as will be shown later, a clear set of rules cannot be established.

Three types of tests are carried out on food additives. First, relatively large doses are fed, of the order of 1–5 per cent of the diet (that is, 100–1000 times as much as would be used in foods). This is to establish how toxic the substance is. All substances are harmful at high doses, but substances toxic at the lower end of the dose range would be ruled out without proceeding any further.

Secondly, if it is a relatively harmless substance, the additive is fed at varying dose levels for longer periods (90 days is the usual time) and the animals are then examined for as many types of change as possible—growth, amount of food eaten, and the condition of the blood and the liver, kidneys, heart, and adrenal glands. In fact, every organ and tissue is examined, including a large number of enzymes and everything else that can serve as an index of change.

Thirdly, long-term feeding trials are continued for $1\frac{1}{2}$–2 years, in order to rule out cancer-producing substances. To cover the possibility that there may be different effects on different types of animals, the tests are carried out on three different species. Tests are also carried out on the male sperm and during the reproductive cycle, to find whether the infant in the womb can be harmed.

After all these results have been collated, the final decision is still far from clear; it is a matter of scientific opinion and common sense. Since almost everything is toxic at a high dose level, what level of the tested substance is to be permitted in foods? Other things have to be taken into account: some foods may be eaten more frequently or in larger amounts than others, and some substances may be used in several different foods. Both these factors will increase the amount of additive likely to be consumed.

The usual practice is to feed the substance to an experimental animal at higher and higher dose levels in a 90-day test, until some effect is observed. The dose just below this amount, that is, the highest no-effect dose, is picked out, and the amount permitted in food is usually one-hundredth of this. Thus there would be a safety factor of 100.

This cannot be a hard-and-fast rule, since, for example, salt is already commonly eaten in amounts well above this safety margin. Similarly, if a food is eaten in rather small amounts, there is no need for such a large safety margin. Or if people have eaten the substance for many years with no apparent effect, it may be decided that there is no need for such a large safety margin. Factors of this kind would be a better guide on the whole than extrapolation from animal experiments.

Foods eaten commonly by children must have a greater safety factor, or if there is inadequate scientific control in the factories (as may occur in some countries), then the safety margin must be increased. The impossibility of making hard-and-fast rules explains why a chemical allowed in one country may be banned in another. Cyclamate, the artificial sweetener, was banned in the United States and Great Britain after very large doses had been shown to cause cancer in a very small number of rats after 2 years of feeding. However, there is no evidence that any human being anywhere in the world has ever suffered any harm from cyclamate. Several other countries have continued to permit the sale of foods sweetened with cyclamate. This illustrates the difficulty of reaching an honest and safe decision.

The problem is further illustrated by changes in regulations applying to food colours. The Colouring Matter in Foods Regulations of 1957 introduced the first list of permitted colouring agents in Great Britain (until then there was only a prohibited list). The permitted list contained 30 synthetic dyes and 19 natural colours. The list was revised in 1966 when 6 dyes were deleted and 1 new one and 3 new natural colours added. In 1970 a further colour was removed from the list. The change proposed in the 1973 regulations was to harmonize British regulations with those of the Common Market, and some dyes were deleted and others added to make a list of 22 dyes and 18 natural colours. However, despite the combined scientific knowledge and food technology of the nine European countries there is still a major difference between the colouring agents permitted in Europe and in the United States—there are only 5 dyes out of the 22 common to both trading areas.

From time to time substances are removed from the list of permitted chemical additives, on the basis of suspicion and lack of certainty about safety. The flour bleacher, agene (nitrogen trichloride), was banned in 1950 because flour treated with it caused running fits in dogs, but there is no evidence whether or not it affects human beings. Brominated oils (as the name implies, oils that have been treated with bromine) were once used in fruit squashes to stop the flavouring oils floating to the top of the bottle. They were banned in 1967 when bromine was found in the body fat of children in countries using these products. There was no evidence of any harm, but the obvious rule is 'better safe than sorry'.

IS IT WORTH THE RISK?

Since the problems are so difficult to resolve, and if it is impossible to prove the negative requirement that the additives be harmless, then we might well ask why we do not ban them altogether and eat unprocessed, natural foods.

There are two reasons why we do not. First, society balances usefulness against risk. To be logical we should ban motor cars since so many people are killed because of them; gas and electricity should be banned for similar reasons. But society has decided that their value outweighs the harm they cause. Similarly with good additives; they are useful, some are essential, and the risk is doubtful. But if there is any recognizable risk, the additive is not permitted in any country that exercises food controls.

The second reason is that the alternative, the consumption only of unprocessed foods, provides no guarantee of safety either. Most fruits and vegetables contain measurable amounts of known toxic substances. This is not a case of doubtful possibility of harmfulness but of known poisons. Cassava or manioc root contains cyanide, as does the Yugoslavian liqueur, slivovitz. Cabbages and all members of that family contain substances that cause goitre (goitrogens), and many peas and beans contain substances that interfere with the digestive enzymes (trypsin inhibitors). Everyone knows that rhubarb leaves are poisonous because they contain oxalic acid, but so do the parts we eat (the stems), and so does tea. Even peanuts contain some poisons.

The operative word is, of course, 'some'. These foods cannot be very toxic otherwise we could not survive. They do, however, contain significant amounts of poisons, and some people do die, for example, from eating improperly prepared cassava. Just over 2 kg of rhubarb contains a fatal dose of oxalic acid, and so the legal safe dose would be less than 25 g of rhubarb a day! (one-hundredth of the highest no-effect dose).

The problem that gives rise to concern about all these chemicals, natural and synthetic, is whether a small dose causes a small degree of harm. It may take 10 kg of cabbage to produce goitre in an adult man, but can the ordinary portion cause a small amount of damage?

Millions of people eat potatoes in very large quantities, but it is possible to be poisoned by potatoes, and many cases have been reported in the medical literature. There was an outbreak in Glasgow in 1917 in which 61 people became

ill and one died. Four people fell ill in a small outbreak
in 1959. A hotel proprietor and four members of his family
ate cold meat and potatoes; the proprietor ate only the flesh
of the potatoes and was not affected, but the members of
the family who ate the skin fell ill.

The cause of the toxicity of the potatoes is the alkaloid,
solanine, which is present in small amounts in all potatoes
but occasionally can be present in toxic amounts. The
average amount present is 8 mg in 100 g of potato, compared
with the toxic dose for man of 20–25 mg (not much of a
safety margin). In the four cases described above the
potatoes were unusual in that they contained 50 mg per
100 g of potato. The solanine content is higher in the skin
of the potato and in green parts that have been exposed to
light.

While it is not the author's intention to frighten people
about potatoes—millions of people eat them regularly
without any harm—the example emphasizes the impossibility of dividing foods into harmful processed or harmless
natural ones. In fact we apply more stringent regulations
to manufactured foods than nature does to natural ones.
The manufacturer must demonstrate that the additives
are needed and that it is safe to use them, and the amounts
permitted are controlled by law in most countries. If
Columbus arrived in Europe today with his first shipment
of potatoes, it is unlikely that they would be admitted.

We have, of course, eaten these foods for thousands of
years and man is still here to debate the issue. We take
regular doses of goitrogens, cyanogens, solanine, and the
rest, without apparent harm. Of course, we do not know
whether we would live longer or better if we stopped eating
them, but there would be little to eat.

The answer to the problem of how we manage to survive
probably lies in the detoxicating mechanism of the body.
When poisons are ingested they go to the liver, where they
are chemically changed so that they can be excreted from
the body. Only when the amount taken is large enough,
or the toxin is one that the body has no biochemical
machinery to deal with, does death result. So whether the

small doses of poison are supplied by nature or by man, we probably metabolize and excrete them. In this respect, the man-made ones appear to be little different from the natural ones. Tables 6.1 and 6.2 show the apparently

TABLE 6.1

Ingredients

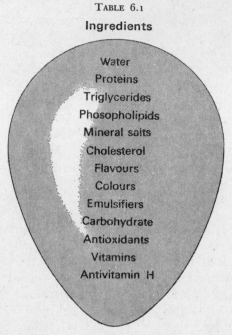

Water
Proteins
Triglycerides
Phosopholipids
Mineral salts
Cholesterol
Flavours
Colours
Emulsifiers
Carbohydrate
Antioxidants
Vitamins
Antivitamin H

n.b. The packaging material is not to be eaten

frightening chemicals that occur in the 'natural' foods, eggs and tomatoes.

WHAT IS 'NATURAL'?

Without knowing anything about the presence of toxins in many fresh, unprocessed foods, there is a vague feeling in many people's minds—elevated to the realms of proven fact by some individuals—that 'natural' foods are good for us, and, in contrast, anything that may be described as synthetic, substitute, or artificial is harmful.

In fact it is difficult to decide whether any foods can be

TABLE 6.2

Substances identified in the smell of fresh tomatoes

Methyl salicylate	Acetaldehyde
2-Phenylethanol	Acetic acid
p-Ethylphenol	Propionic acid
trans-6-methyl-3,5-Heptadiene	γ-Butyrolactone
2-one	2-Butanol-3-one
3,5-Heptadiene-2-one	Isovaleraldehyde
6-Methyl-5-heptene-2-one	1-Pentene-3-ol
γ-Octalactone	Isovaleric acid
Caprilic acid	2-Methylbutyric acid
p-Vinylguaiacol	2-Methyl-1-butanol
γ-Nonalactone	Phenol
2,6,6-trimethyl-2-hydroxy-	*trans*, *trans*-2,4-Hexadienal
2-cyclohexanone	*trans*-2-Hexenal
Eugenol	*cis*-3-Hexenal
trans, *trans*-2,4-Decadienal	ξ-Caprolactone
Linalool	Hexanal
2,6,6-Trimethyl-2-hydroxy	*cis*-3-Hexene-1-ol
cyclohexylidene acetic acid	1-Hexanol
lactone	Benzaldehyde
β-Ionone	Salicylaldehyde
5,6-Epoxyionone	Benzyl alcohol
Geranylacetone	*o*-Cresol
2-Isobutylthiazole	Guaiacol
Phenylacetonitrile	*trans*, *trans*-2,4-Heptadienal
Phenylacetaldehyde	*trans*, *cis*-2,4-Heptadienal
o-Hydroxyacetophenone	

considered as being 'natural' for man. The only one that can be so described is mothers' milk, still considered the ideal food for babies, despite the proliferation of specially prepared infant foods. After babyhood there is no reason to believe that any one food is more 'natural' for man than any other.

What is often meant by the term 'natural' is unprocessed food still in its natural state. Thus the old dish, frumenty, is often offered as a 'natural' boon of special value to health. Frumenty consists of the whole-wheat grain soaked in water until it swells and bursts, and then boiled in milk. By the same argument, if the processing were carried out in the factory and frumenty were made available in cans, this would no longer be a 'natural' food.

There is a belief that whole food, like the whole-wheat grain, is man's natural food, in contrast with the white flour, from which 30 per cent of the grain has been removed. If whole food is the aim, then it would be logical, even if indigestible, to eat the stalks and roots of the plant as well. Certainly the whole grain, or the wholemeal bread made from it, is more nutritious than white bread, since part of the nutrients have been discarded in the making of white bread. But there is nothing 'natural' about the wheat grain as a food for man, whole or extracted. The natural function of the wheat grain is to produce another wheat plant, not to feed man. Wheat grain, as other foods, was found accidentally rather than as a result of a systematic search by man for the most nutritious and attractive foods provided by nature. In his early days of wandering the face of the earth, man came across the wild wheat plant and tasted it and found it good. Later he cultivated the crop and improved the yield and quality. Wheat is, however, a relatively recent introduction into man's menu. Until he settled down only about 10 000 years ago, he hunted meat and ate wild berries and roots, so wheat is a new food and man is not necessarily well adapted to consume it—whether brown or white.

Health foods

So it is possible to rave about the 'good old days' when man was close to nature, without a shred of evidence that his diet was nutritionally preferable. Still, the hankering after nature persists, explaining the vogue of 'health foods', which is a reaction to pollution, industrialization, and other man-made problems. There is no general definition of 'health foods', but there are several types of foods sold in what are called 'health food shops'. Some are good, some are reasonable and honest, but others are fairly straightforward swindles.

Health foods can be defined as substances whose consumption is promoted by various food-reform movements. They include: (a) vegetarian foods, since some but certainly not all, addicts are vegetarians; (b) whole-grain cereals; (c) foods grown in soil enriched with plant compost or animal manure without the use of inorganic fertilizers and without the use of pesticides and weedkillers; (d) foods processed without the use of chemical additives, often incorrectly called unprocessed foods; (e) 'magical' foods, like honey, sea salt, yogurt, molasses, buckwheat, and vitamin E; and (f) pills, potions, and elixirs that have no value whatever but are widely acclaimed as cures for everything suffered by mankind. It is clear from such a catalogue that it is not possible to discuss the pros and cons of health foods as a whole; we must consider each type separately.

Possibly half the population of the world is vegetarian, although largely from necessity rather than choice. Meat and fish are not essential to the diet, and vegetarians can be (and usually are) just as healthy as carnivores and omnivores. It is possible to live well as a vegan (a person who eats no animal food at all and so shuns milk and eggs). It is even possible to go farther as do the Jains of India, who eat no food that grows below the ground as well as being lacto-vegetarians. To those who like their meat it seems impossible to live without it, but certainly Jains can be as well fed as anyone else.

Whole-grain cereals are more nutritious than extracted cereals, and brown bread is better than white—it has slightly more protein, more iron, more bran, and more of several vitamins—but this does not mean that people living on white bread (whether or not fortified with added nutrients such as B vitamins, calcium, and iron) are poorer in health. We do not live on single foods, but eat a wide variety of foods when we can get them, so it is not essential to eat brown bread even if the nutritionist does say that it is better for you. Many people prefer the taste of white bread, it keeps longer, and some people have difficulty in dealing with all the bran present in wholemeal. Even the nutritionist finally admits that people eat what they like rather than what is good for them.

There are several reform movements that advocate foods grown in compost or manure, although the natural food for the plant is inorganic salts. Despite years of research, no one has shown that foods organically manured are nutri-

tionally superior to any other, nor do they taste any different
to most of the people who have tasted them in the few
published trials that have been carried out. The use of
pesticides and weedkillers is, of course, a compromise
between losing part of our crops and adding traces of unwanted chemicals into our food. The fact that most countries
exercise some degree of control over their use, particularly
of pesticides, indicates that we would do without them if
we could. But once again, in helping to increase our much-
needed food supply, they are not as totally evil as health-
food addicts would have us think. The use of chemical
additives in processing has already been discussed. Certainly
there is always a risk in consuming unnecessary chemicals
but, apart from a few speciality foods made for a smaller
market and costing more to buy, it does not seem possible
to do without them.

The main criticism of health-food shops is the un-
warranted claims that are made for magical foods and pills
and potions. Honey, because it has a long history, has
carried its magic into the twentieth century and has been
declared a cure-all. In fact it is very like sugar in its composition. Sugar is a chemical combination of glucose and
fructose; honey is a solution of the two separate sugars.
Honey has small traces of several other chemicals and only
traces of vitamins. In the amounts that most people could
eat without being sick it makes no practical contribution
to the diet except as a source of empty calories, like sugar.
Presumably on the same basis as whole foods, brown sugar is
praised above white, but it differs hardly at all from the
pure, white sucrose, whether extracted from sugar cane,
beet, or palm. The traces of impurities in honey and brown
sugar give them a pleasant taste, but they supply no significant nutrients. Plenty of statements to the contrary can be
found in popular magazines and health-food literature, but
they are quite untrue.

Likewise, because stainless steel has superseded copper
in jam boilers, nostalgia for the good old days makes health-
food addicts buy more expensive 'hand-filled pots of jam
made in copper vessels'. In fact, such jam will contain no

vitamin C whatever since it is completely destroyed by traces of copper.

Worse still are the magical pills and potions. Simple substances like table salt sold under the ancient name of natrium muriate, or sulphate of calcium (known in other shops as plaster of Paris), or esoteric remedies such as garlic and herbal extracts are all claimed to cure backache or front ache, clear the bowels and arteries, and lead to a long and healthy old age.

If these were the foods eaten in the 'good old days', one might ask why our forefathers died so young and why people today live so much longer. Any innocent, fool, or charlatan can make his claim; then he leaves it to the scientist to 'disprove' it. Few scientists are willing to give up their current work to investigate unsubstantiated claims, and so these magical elixirs continue to sell to ever-optimistic consumers.

7

Diet and disease

In its early history the science of nutrition was based mostly on the investigation of deficiency diseases and led to a knowledge of the nutrients required by man. This might be termed the first stage in the development of the science, since the emphasis has changed in recent years. It now concerns itself with more complex problems relating diet to disease, including the relation between diet and non-dietary factors in our environment.

Obvious deficiency diseases have almost completely disappeared from Western countries, and the nutritional state of the general population appears to be excellent with regard to the rarity of scurvy, beri-beri, pellagra, and the like. However, there are some possible problems remaining in the area of what might be termed old-fashioned nutrition because of people's widely differing eating habits. While the average intake of all nutrients is well above the average needs, there is no guarantee that some people at the lower end of the range are not suffering from a shortage. There are people who restrict their diet to relatively few foods because of personal likes or fads and so may have a low intake of some particular nutrient. There are also those who 'slim' over-enthusiastically and so limit their intake of all nutrients. There are teenagers who subsist largely on snacks and those who dilute an adequate diet with 'empty calories'. None of these groups shows any obvious signs of nutritional deficiency, but their low nutrient intake places them at possible risk. Firmer evidence comes from the finding that children from the lower socio-economic groups grow more slowly than the average and one of the reasons for this appears to be a poorer diet (Table 7.1).

TABLE 7.1

Heights and weights relative to social class
(expressed as percentage of average for the same age)

	School	Height	Weight
Boys	Secondary modern	99·1	99·3
	Grammar	103·3	103·2
	Royal Naval College	106·2	106·5
Girls	Secondary modern	98·9	99·4
	Grammar	104·2	103·6

(From Sutcliffe and Canham (1950). *Heights and weights of children.*)

Deficiency diseases, however, are much less significant in the Western population than the newer 'diseases of affluence'. A number of diseases have appeared or greatly increased in the West within one or two generations. Because they have appeared at a time of rising standards of living they have been termed 'diseases of affluence', and some appear to be related to diet. The complicating factor is that many other, non-dietary, factors are undoubtedly involved so that it is extremely difficult to isolate the dietary causes.

HEART DISEASE

Perhaps the best example is coronary heart disease. This is certainly a disease of affluence—it is rare and even unknown in many primitive and developing communities. Deaths from heart disease have increased in Great Britain from 800 per million men in 1930 to eight times that rate in 1974; it is more common among the richer. In some of the poorer countries it is unknown in the villages, and yet is a major cause of death in the big cities.

The problem is to find what factors are common under

these different conditions. It is known that heart disease is commoner among people who smoke, take little exercise, have high blood-pressure, are overweight, and suffer what is generally termed 'stress'. Diet is also involved, but it is clearly only one factor (or possibly four factors) among many, and to complicate the picture thoroughly, heredity plays an important part in the disease. However, if diet is involved at least we can attempt to remove that cause. The reason for saying that there are, possibly, four dietary factors is that fats, sugar, hard water, and fibre have all been implicated. But so far little is proven and there is plenty of room for argument.

The suggestion that fat is implicated arises because animal fats like lard, butter, and meat fat increase the levels of particular types of fats found normally in the blood, including cholesterol and triglycerides. When a person has a heart attack the levels of these fats in his blood are abnormally high, and the communities where animal fats are eaten in fairly large amounts are those where heart disease is common. Although this is certainly a long way from proving that animal fats cause any harm, the findings are regarded as being more than suggestive.

Many vegetable oils (those containing a particular type of fat called 'polyunsaturates') can reduce the level of the cholesterol in the blood. Whether or not this is beneficial in preventing heart disease is difficult to prove. The oils that contain polyunsaturates include sunflower, soya-bean, and cottonseed (not olive oil), and the margarines made from them. There have been large-scale experiments in which people have replaced the animal fats in their diet with vegetable oils, and foods like biscuits and cheese which are rich in ordinary fat have been specially made with these polyunsaturates. In some experiments there was some improvement in heart conditions, but they provide no clear proof of the benefits of polyunsaturates.

Sugar has been cast in the role of the villain partly because a large increase in sugar consumption has run parallel with the increase in heart disease. A hundred years ago sugar was a very small part of the diet; just over 10 kg per person per year was consumed in 1850 in Great Britain; now the figure is 55 kg per person per year, on average. World sugar consumption has trebled since 1900. In the United States the average sugar consumption has increased by 120 per cent since the end of the last century, while fat consumption has increased by only 12 per cent.

A second count against sugar is that many manufactured foods like cakes, biscuits, and chocolates contain both sugar and fats, so that any blame attached to fats as a dietary cause of disease could equally well be attached to sugar. Unfortunately there have been no large-scale experiments in which people have given up sugar, so that the evidence is far from complete.

The fibre story is more recent, dating from about 1970. It arose from observations that communities who ate a relatively large amount of fibre in the form of cereal bran—that is, whole wheat and brown rice as opposed to white flour and polished rice—had little or no heart disease. However, the evidence is rather thin.

The hard-water theory arose in Great Britain. People living in areas where the water is hard have a lower incidence of heart disease than in areas where it is soft. The observation has not yet been explained.

Apart from the fact that heart disease is caused by a multiplicity of factors and that diet may be only one of these, it is possible that individuals may respond differently to these suspected foods. Direct experimentation has, so far, provided only limited information. Very large numbers of experiments have been carried out in which changes in the blood fats have been measured following specific changes in the foods eaten. These have included replacing animal fats with one of the vegetable fats, replacing sucrose with starch, removing any one of a large range of foods from the diet, or adding one or more thought to be beneficial. Such experiments can rarely be continued for more than a few weeks because of the difficulty in persuading volunteers to continue much longer as guinea-pigs (even when they are paid), whereas in real life it may well take many years of eating the suspected food before there is a permanent change in the blood fats or before any danger results.

Finally, to make clear the problems of the nutritionist in this field, factors such as exercise or worry and stress can also change the levels of fats in the blood. All this explains why it is very misleading when any single finding is heralded as a cause or cure for diseases of this complicated type. Scientific research involves many thousands of observations, sifted and re-examined repeatedly before a clear pattern emerges, and facts taken out of context can cause false alarms or raise false hopes.

The paucity of firm evidence is illustrated by the lack of agreement in the medical world on what advice should be offered to the public. In seven countries of the Western world, medical experts advise members of the public to increase their consumption of polyunsaturated fats, but the official opinion in Great Britain is that there is not sufficient evidence on which to base such advice. All do agree, however, that it would probably be an advantage to reduce our intake of fat as a whole—in Great Britain the average person takes in 40–45 per cent of his energy as fat.

The advice offered by the American Heart Association is: (a) reduce fat intake to 30–35 per cent of the energy intake; (b) restrict animal fats to less than 10 per cent of the energy intake; (c) increase polyunsaturates to 11–14 per cent of the energy intake; and (d) reduce dietary cholesterol to less than 300 mg per day, that is, not more than three egg yolks per week. It is also recommended in Great Britain as well as in the United States that sugar intake should be reduced.

It is clearly also desirable to reduce the risk by modifying smoking, increasing exercise, and reducing body weight. However, all these suggestions must be regarded as precautions. There is no firm evidence that they are more than that.

DIETARY FIBRE AND DISEASES OF THE BOWEL

One method of examining the causes of ill-health, termed epidemiology, is to observe the habits and disease patterns

of large numbers of people living under a variety of conditions. Unfortunately, the results sometimes lead the ob-
server astray. For example, it has been observed that people
living in Central Africa consume a lot of cereal fibre in
their diet and do not suffer from certain diseases of the
bowel (diverticular disease), which are very common in
Europe. These two facts may or may not be related. Not
only is the food of the African native very different from that
of the European, but his whole way of life is different—
ranging from freedom from petrol fumes to freedom from
income tax. The epidemiologist is faced with the observations and has to find out whether or not they are causally
related, which is a very different matter.

The following diseases have been found to occur together
(that is, they are either all common or all absent in different
types of community): heart disease, cancer of the large
intestine, obesity, diseases of the bowel, diabetes, appendi-
citis, gallstones and varicose veins. Communities that have
these diseases on the whole eat white bread, which is low
in fibre; communities that do not have the diseases eat a
variety of whole-grain cereals that are rich in fibre. But
the two types of communities differ also in so many other
factors that dietary differences are difficult to evaluate.

However, doctors have recently cured patients of diverticular disease by giving them bran to eat, whereas previously
the disease was treated by sieving all fibrous materials out
of their foods. Whether this successful treatment provides
evidence that these diseases are caused by a diet low in
fibre is difficult to decide until more evidence comes to
light.

Meanwhile, the layman wants to know if he should eat
brown bread which is rich in fibre rather than white bread.
The answer is yes, even if the advice is regarded only as an
insurance policy should the protagonists of this theory be
proved right. Apart from diseases of the bowel, bran has
been advocated for many years to prevent constipation.
Furthermore, there are more B vitamins, minerals, and a
little more protein in wholemeal bread. (Wholemeal bread
consists of the whole wheat grain. When 5 per cent of the

bran is sieved out, the product is '95 per cent extraction flour' and the loaf is called wheatmeal. Both are commonly called brown bread. White bread has 30 per cent of the grain removed and is made from '70 per cent extraction flour' with little fibre in it.) Whatever nutritionists say, about 90 per cent of all bread sold is white. Throughout the world and throughout the ages there has been a preference for refined white bread, and judging by bread sales, most people still prefer it.

DIET AND MENTAL DISORDERS

There are a number of disorders in which the patient cannot deal with one or other of the normal foodstuffs, and sometimes disease results. These disorders are known as 'inborn errors of metabolism', since they are present at birth. They can be treated by strict control of the diet. The first such defect was noted in 1906. Since then many hundreds of such diseases have come to light. However, only a very small number of people are involved.

One of the earliest of these inborn disorders to be identified was phenylketonuria, discovered in 1934 in Norway with the aid of an observant mother of two mentally retarded children. In addition to her persistence in searching for treatment, the mother reported a musty smell coming from the children. The physician, Dr. Fölling, examined the children for infection and, when testing the urine, found an unexpected chemical reaction. Together with the mother's information about the smell, this reaction led him to identify an unexpected substance, phenylpyruvic acid, in the urine. He suggested that this was formed from the amino acid phenylalanine, which is part of all protein foods, and which these children could not metabolize normally. The abnormal metabolite affected the brain.

Phenylketonuria is a rare disease which occurs in one in about 12 000 births (about 0·008 per cent), and in the past inevitably led to mental retardation. In mental institutions the incidence is about 1 per cent. The adult is beyond treatment since the brain has been damaged, but if the disease is detected in the first few weeks of life (which it can be by a simple chemical test on the wet napkins or by a blood test) before any damage is done, then strict control of the amount of phenylalanine in the diet allows the child to develop normally. Phenylalanine is an essential amino acid needed, among other purposes, to synthesize tissue proteins. Thus the child must receive some in his diet, but only enough for essential purposes, as any surplus would be converted into the dangerous metabolite.

Other diseases of similar type, also rare, have been found, where a nutrient that is essential cannot be properly metabolized and so must be very carefully restricted in the diet. Special dietary preparations, together with foods very low in the amounts of the offending substance, have to be used.

A comparable disorder is one on which the child cannot make use of milk sugar. This was first observed in 1958. The problem is solved simply by keeping milk sugar out of the diet. Several similar conditions are now recognized, which leads to the hope that more of the diseases of mankind may be controlled by dietary means.

OBESITY

The area of nutrition in which many people are most deeply interested is that generally defined as 'slimming'. In conversation it is a subject as popular as the weather, and is discussed with about the same degree of knowledge; that is, everyone can see the end result, but no one knows why it happens. In Great Britain about £40 million is spent annually on 'slimming foods'. At any given moment about a fifth of the population are 'dieting', taking drugs, or buying mechanical devices to aid slimming.

Everyone has a store of fat under the skin and around the vital organs; it serves as a food reserve, for heat insulation, and to protect the vital organs from physical damage. In many people it amounts to one-tenth or one-fifth of the total body weight, and the amount stays fairly constant. In other people, it can amount to a quarter, a half, or even three-quarters of the total body weight, and it increases continually.

It is only in recent years that the problem of obesity has become widely recognized as a medical problem. Before that it was something of a joke, except to those afflicted with the disease—for a disease it is now accepted to be. The problems of the fat person are many: increased risk of diabetes, heart disease, gout, high blood-pressure, bronchitis, gallstones, and varicose veins. Fat people are at greater risk in surgery and childbirth, they have a higher accident rate, and, finally, their lives are shorter.

According to figures collected by the United States Society of Actuaries from large numbers of subjects, men who are 10 per cent overweight have a 13 per cent increased death risk. This rises to 25 per cent if they are 20 per cent overweight, and to 42 per cent if they are 30 per cent overweight. For women the increased death risk is 9 per cent for 10 per cent overweight, 21 per cent for 20 per cent overweight, and 30 per cent for 30 per cent overweight.

Put another way, a man over 45 who is 11 kg (25 lb) overweight reduces his life expectancy by 25 per cent—he is likely to die at 60 instead of 80. If he loses his surplus weight, his life expectation returns almost to normal. American studies have shown that men who were 25 per cent or more overweight and had an increased expectation of death of 28 per cent reduced this risk to 9 per cent when they regained their normal weight. A group of men who were 35–40 per cent overweight had an expected mortality rate 51 per cent greater than average, and this fell dramatically almost exactly to 'normal' when they lost their surplus weight.

Most fat people know that they are fat by looking at themselves. What they want to know is how much they are overweight. The problem really is the amount of fat in the body, although weight is usually an adequate index. It is possible for an athlete to develop enough muscle to put him in the overweight class, but he may not be carrying excess fat. If anyone really wants to measure the fat in the body— and research workers often do—the subject has to be weighed both in air and submerged in water, as did Archimedes with the royal crown. After making due allowance for the air left in the lungs, the fat is calculated from the density of the body. A short cut is to measure the fat lying under the skin by pinching the skin and measuring the thickness. If this is measured as several specified sites, the body fat can be calculated. The method is not very reliable, because the fat can be distributed unevenly over different parts of the body.

Weight is a much simpler index of fat, but it has to be compared with some standard. Averages are of little use since most people tend to gain weight between the ages of 20 and 50, whereas better health is maintained if we stay at whatever weight we were at age 20, unless of course it was excessive at that time. The insurance companies, who have a vested interest in the health of their clients, have drawn up tables of 'desirable' body weights, which are related to height and do not change with age (Table 7.2). These are based on very large numbers of people, and anyone whose weight is 10 per cent above the desirable weight for his or her height is at risk.

There is no perfect body weight and no precise standard. The weights shown in the tables cover a range. A scientist studying the behaviour pattern of fat people suggested that one method of designating fat people is those who automatically select the maximum weight for height rather than being fair and selecting the middle value.

Body frames pose another difficult problem. The tables show small, medium, and large frames. This is probably the only practical approach, but there are many more frame sizes and certainly no sudden jump from small to medium to large: there are gradations from the smallest to the largest.

Why do some people get fat?

The reason some people get fat is that they are out of energy balance. That is, they consume more energy as food than they use, and the surplus is converted into reserve stores

TABLE 7.2

Height–weight tables: weight in pounds according to frame (in indoor clothing—estimated men 7–9 lb; women 4–6 lb). For girls between 18 and 25 subtract 1 lb for each year under 25

Desirable weights for men, aged 25 and over				Desirable weights for women, aged 25 and over			
Height (without shoes) ft in	Small frame	Medium frame	Large frame	Height (without shoes) ft in	Small frame	Medium frame	Large frame
5 1	112–120	118–129	126–141	4 8	92–98	96–107	104–119
5 2	115–123	121–123	129–144	4 9	94–101	98–110	106–122
5 3	118–126	124–136	132–148	4 10	96–104	101–113	
5 4	121–129	127–139	135–152	4 11	99–107	104–116	112–128
5 5	124–133	130–143	138–156	5 0	102–110	107–119	115–131
5 6	128–137	134–147	142–161	5 1	105–113	110–122	118–134
5 7	132–141	138–152	147–166	5 2	108–116	113–126	121–138
5 8	136–145	142–156	151–170	5 3	111–119	116–130	125–142
5 9	140–150	146–160	155–174	5 4	114–123	120–135	129–146
5 10	144–154	150–165	159–179	5 5	118–127	124–139	133–150
5 11	148–158	154–170	164–184	5 6	122–131	128–143	137–154
6 0	152–162	158–175	168–189	5 7	126–135	132–147	141–158
6 1	156–167	162–180	173–194	5 8	130–140	136–151	145–163
6 2	160–171	167–185	178–199	5 9	134–144	140–155	149–168
6 3	164–175	172–190	182–204	5 10	138–148	144–159	153–173

To convert these figures into kilograms, a rough estimate may be obtained by dividing by 2 (actually 2·205), for example, a small-framed woman, height 4 ft 8 in should weigh between 46 kg and 48 kg.
1 ft=0·3 m.
From Metropolitan Life Insurance Co.

known as adipose tissue. These reserves are not always in the most welcome places.

Energy balance is simply the difference between intake and output. Anyone who maintains constant body weight, and very many people do, must be balancing the equation, although we are not sure how it is done. The amount of food eaten will often depend on its attractiveness and a host of other psychological and social factors—attractive surroundings and sweet music will always encourage us to eat more. Our energy intake will also depend not only on the amount of food eaten but upon the kind of food. It may

be bulky food, low in energy, such as most fruits and vegetables, or it may be highly concentrated in energy, like fats
and sugar-rich foods; so that amount of food intake and the
energy intake are not necessarily correlated.

Apart from these outside factors we have some unknown
mechanism for internally controlling appetite. Some device
tells us when to eat and when to stop eating. Numerous
theories have been put forward, all with some evidence, but
none is satisfactory. The theories include a postulation of
an appetite centre and a satiety centre in the brain, which
are possibly controlled by the levels of sugar in the blood,
or the difference between the sugar in the blood entering
and leaving the organs, or skin temperature, or blood-levels
of fatty acids. Another theory suggests that there is a metabolite that partitions itself between fat stores and other
parts of the body, so that the amount of fat is itself a controlling mechanism.

Experimental animals are not much help in appetite
studies, because whatever physiological and biochemical
mechanisms they reveal seem to be rather easily overcome
in man by factors such as palatability, prestige, and social
conditions. Certainly the behaviourists have shown major
differences between fat and thin people in the strength and
importance of these factors specific to man.

It seems possible that thin people keep thin because they
burn off any surplus food eaten, and that fat people gain
weight because they do not have this facility. Perhaps they
should be thought of as being more efficient, since they do
not waste their food.

Some factors can affect both intake and output. For
example, cold weather can increase heat output and also
appetite, as can exercise. Whatever the control mechanism,
the simple fact remains that anyone who is gaining weight
is consuming more energy than he or she is using.

Some people are 'hearty eaters', some describe themselves
as 'pigs'—they eat all they can see and love their food more
than their health. Others may get fat, not because they
eat excessively (they may even eat less than the average),

but because their energy expenditure is so low that they are still eating more than they are using.

How can the surplus be lost?

The logical deduction from what has been said above about energy balance is that fat will be lost when the energy balance becomes negative. This can be done either by eating less or exercising more. It is a simple arithmetic problem, but difficult advice to follow. Difficult because most people find it very hard indeed to limit their food intake, and because the amount of energy spent in exercise is very little in terms of the weight of body fat.

One kilogram of body fat contains about 7500 kcal. A whole week's food intake for an average adult (say 2500 kcal per day) is 17 500 kcal. So if the food intake were cut by 10 per cent, saving 1750 kcal, it would still take 2 weeks to lose ½ kg. It is difficult to burn off excess weight by exercise largely because about two-thirds of the total daily expenditure of energy is for basal purposes, so any extra exercise involves only the remaining third. A bright idea might be to walk a fast couple of kilometres every evening after dinner to burn off some of your body fat—it will, but only about 12 g. And if you stop at the local public house for a pint of beer on the way don't have more than half a pint, otherwise the imbalance between extra output from all that walking and input from the little drinking will result in a weight *gain*.

Where exercise is most effective is in stopping you getting fat in the first place. A 10-minute brisk walk may take only 100 kcal, so it would take 75 brisk walks to lose 1 kg of weight! On the other hand, the same walk could stop you gaining weight. If you eat 100 kcal more than you need— only one slice of bread with butter or a pint of beer—you could gain ½ kg in 35 days, 5 kg in a year, 100 kg (15 stone) between the ages of 20 and 40. A 10-minute walk daily could prevent this. This of course assumes that the body is acting like a bank account without the charges, which may not be true at all times, but it does illustrate the usefulness of even a little regular exercise in keeping weight down, compared with the insignificance of exercise in getting rid of surplus weight.

So to get rid of body fat we must eat less. To the nutritionist, less means fewer calories. It may not mean the same to the ordinary consumer, since he wants to fill his mouth and stomach, but it is possible to design a diet that is low in calories and still adequate in attraction, palatability, and bulk, so the subject does not feel deprived.

There are many gimmicks available, including drugs. Some slimming aids are useless, but some do help to control appetite or to stimulate metabolism, so that the body burns off more of the fat reserves. The problem, apart from the many side-effects of the drugs, is what you do when you stop taking these 'crutches'. Most people return to the very eating habits that caused obesity in the first place. That is why, although some doctors use drugs as aids, the only effective way of losing weight and keeping it down is by learning better eating habits and sticking to them for life. This is extremely difficult for a person who likes food more than health, figure, or pocket, and who expects immediate results. If it took five or ten years to get fat why should it go in a week? The control of eating habits by learning, cajoling, and understanding the special problems of fat people, and at the same time making sure that the subject is getting all the nutrients required, is the only long-term solution.

The worst possible thing that people can do, and they often do it, is to half-starve themselves. When they are put on, say, a 1500-kcal diet, they boast of eating only half this amount, or less. The nutrients that the body requires for good health come from our food; if the diet is properly constructed it is just possible to get all the nutrients from a diet of 1200–1500 kcal, but certainly not from a diet of much less than this. So people who starve or half-starve themselves are undermining their health. That is why we are told not to slim by ourselves, but to take advice from our doctors, who nowadays are receiving the necessary training in nutrition.

8

Two blades of grass

The most urgent problem facing the human race is how to feed itself in the coming years. The population is outstripping the food supply. Among the many possibilities of increasing production, the following demonstrate the current developments in a wide range of sciences: (a) improved feeding of plants and animals; (b) improved breeding of plants and animals; (c) better methods of farming the seas; (d) direct consumption of primary foodstuffs; (e) substitute foods; (f) factory production of 'single-cell protein foods'; (g) making edible substances from non-food sources; and (h) synthetic foodstuffs.

IMPROVED FEEDING OF PLANTS AND ANIMALS

Agricultural developments over recent generations have included the improved feeding of plants (the use of fertilizers). Nitrogen, potassium, and phosphate have been known as plant nutrients for a long time, but recent work has been devoted to the types and amounts used, and the time and methods of application. However the supply of fertilizers is linked with chemical factory production, and the unavailability as well as the cost have restricted large-scale use to the richer industrialized countries. Fertilizers have developed hand in hand with mechanization, the use of pesticides, weed killers and soil conditioners, and other improvements in crop production.

The improved feeding of animals has been achieved as a result of nutrition research. While much of the laboratory experimentation on animals is aimed at improving human nutrition, some part of it has been devoted to the nutrition of the domestic animals themselves. In fact, human nutritionists often complain that more money is spent on animal nutrition than on human nutrition. This is true, simply because there is great profit to be made from improvements in animal nutrition. If a better balance of nutrients or more protein or better timing of feeding can increase the yield of milk, meat, eggs, or wool, even by a small amount, then the research shows a profit. We now know fairly precisely not only the nutritional needs of the domestic chicken but the differing needs for early, rapid growth, for later, slower growth, and for egg laying. We also know the needs of cows for growth, for reproduction, and for milk. Improved nutrition, as part of the many improvements in animal husbandry achieved in recent years, has led to the increased production of food.

Living creatures, both plant and animal, differ from one another. Some varieties grow faster, or are more resistant to disease, or produce more offspring, or give a greater yield in return for their food supply. The geneticist can select or even change varieties of plants and animals to achieve these ends. Improvement through breeding is not new, for farmers have done this with their crops and animals for hundreds of years. What is new is both the science of genetics that allows the process to be carried out more successfully and also the speed of change in recent years. As a result we now have fast-growing 'barley' beef, broiler chickens, varieties of plants that mature earlier or later than before and so lengthen the growing season, and a host of other improvements.

Usually most of these improvements are applied in the Western world long before they can be introduced into the poorer countries. However, one improvement that has been introduced into the developing countries has so dramatic a potential that it has been called the Green Revolution.

The Green Revolution

The Green Revolution began when Dr. Norman Borlaugh of the Rockefeller Foundation, in collaboration with Mexican technicians, discovered high-yield hybrid wheat seeds in Mexico. The Mexican dwarf varieties of wheat, which are insensitive to the day's length and capable of tolerating large fertilizer inputs, yield an average over 15 tonnes per hectare and in some cases over 20 tonnes per hectare. This discovery was followed by high-yield rice varieties. Ordinary rice does not respond well to fertilizers—the leaves grow big and the plants tend to fall over. The new seeds can be sown during any season in the tropics and subtropics, making it possible to use the same land (properly fertilized, irrigated, and seeded) to produce three crops a year.

The use of these high-yield varieties spread rapidly. They were introduced into India in 1966, and in 1968 about $3\frac{1}{2}$ million hectares were sown. It became possible to harvest two crops a year in India—wheat in winter and hybrid maize in summer. A plot of land in Asia which produced 8 tonnes of rice a year now produces 36 tonnes; in 1969 the Philippines became self-sufficient in rice for the first time since 1903; Iran became a rice exporter; in Sri Lanka the crop was 13 per cent greater than ever recorded.

In Mexico, where it all started, between 1943 and 1963 the yield of wheat and maize doubled. Other agricultural developments greatly increased the production of beans, eggs, and chickens. The increased yields were reflected in food consumption. In 1942, 21 million people had only 1700 kcal per day; in 1963, 37 million had 2700 kcal. Between 1953 and 1963, in a world where population was rising about as fast as food supplies, the population of Mexico increased at the extremely fast rate of 3 per cent per year, while the food supply increased at 7 per cent per year.

There are, however, factors other than nutrition and food supplies involved. The new varieties of crops call for greater skill, proper irrigation, and plenty of fertilizers—the type of treatment that can be afforded only by the larger farmer and not by the subsistence peasant. As a result, many peasants have been selling out and moving into the big cities where there are no jobs for them. This is happening all over the world, and in the capital cities the population is increasing at a rate one and a half times as fast as jobs. Even where they have not left the land, the peasant farmers are at a disadvantage. In the early 1970s it was reported that in Pakistan the large farmers were making increased profits, but the landless labourers' incomes had been unchanged for 5 years. The average growth rate of agriculture in Mexico between 1943 and 1963 was so great that the average amount of work available to the labourer fell from 194 to 100 days, and his real income fell by 17 per cent. During the last 10 years of that period, 80 per cent of the increased agricultural production came from 3 per cent of the farms.

The special nature of the high-yield varieties (the need to produce the hybrid seed on a large scale and the high requirements for fertilizer and water) has created problems. These have been greatly intensified by the increase in world oil prices, and their effect on the price and availability of fertilizers.

A report early in 1974 described the complex problems in Punjab, the bread-basket of India. In the last few years the farms and farmers flourished, and the Green Revolution was a great success. Then there developed a severe shortage of diesel fuel, fertilizer, and water, and the quality of the seed deteriorated. When the farmer used bullock power, irrigated from wells, and spread dung or no fertilizer at all, he was not at the mercy of fuel prices and fertilizer supplies. He also used his own seed instead of the new, hybrid variety that has to be bought from the production centre.

At the same time the farmers' financial success made the Government concerned about the formation of a privileged class, even if it was providing food. Two steps were taken: one was to limit the amount of land that any individual could farm (7 hectares of irrigated land or 21 hectares of dry land), and the second was to reduce profits by increasing taxes. The farmers were finding it unprofitable to grow wheat, and the result was a fall in the amount of food being produced.

FARMING THE SEAS

Sea fishing was once compared to collecting butterflies at night—a lucky dip with a large bag. Modern detecting equipment has probably made it a comparison to butterfly collecting at night—with the aid of a candle.

Primitive man hunted his animals; modern man produces them on a farm. Why not do the same with fish? This is the basis of fish farming, whereby large areas of water, such as the lochs in Scotland, are used as feeding grounds. So far this technique has been developed commercially for rainbow trout and salmon but not for the commoner and cheaper fish. Experiments have long been carried out on fertilizing the sea in order to produce a greater food supply for the fish. These experiments were claimed to be successful but have not been developed commercially.

Small-scale fish farming is carried out in fish ponds in many parts of Asia. The pond is stocked with small fish called fingerlings, which grow on the natural and added food supplies. In warm climates they grow to 1 or 2 kg in less than a year, and they provide a useful supplement to the diet. They are also grown in rice fields at the time when the fields are flooded, and the fish are harvested when the field is drained. The fish feed on waste that is thrown into the water, and the excretion of the fish helps to fertilize the rice so the rice yields have increased by 10–20 per cent under such conditions.

However, fish ponds have presented many problems. In the early 1950s great successes were reported with a fish called tilapia, which grew so well in any body of water (ponds, stagnant pools, reservoirs, or lakes) that they were referred to as the mad fish of the Orient—they ate like mad and bred like mad. Twenty years later they were regarded as the bad fish of the Orient: they bred so madly that they did not reach edible size, and they ate so madly that they took the food supply of the native fish. Farming other varieties of fish such as carp has been found to be more successful, and the practice of farming fish is developing in several countries, although slowly.

The resources of the sea

The sea offers a great potential source of food, especially protein-rich foods. By 1950 the commercial fisheries of the world had recovered from wartime problems, and catches amounted to 20 million tonnes a year, of which 85 per cent was used directly as human food. The catch increased to 40 million tonnes by 1960, but only 78 per cent was eaten directly. By 1966 the catch was up to 60 million tonnes, but the proportion eaten directly had fallen to 67 per cent. The remainder was not wasted, since it was converted into fish meal and used for animal protein feed to provide man with meat, milk, and eggs. This process, however, is wasteful compared with eating the fish directly. Fish meal is an extremely rich source of protein, about 70 per cent, with much of the remainder consisting of calcium phosphate from the bones of the fish and, when properly dried in the factory, it has all the nutritive value of fresh fish. It is usually made from three sources: small fish or fish that are not wanted for human food, such as anchovetta of Peru and the menhaden of the United States; waste fish from filleting, and edible fish that are surplus to immediate market needs. There is further potential since up to 50 per cent of the catch is sometimes discarded at sea if the fish are the wrong type for the market.

Fish meal is a coarse powder with an extremely fishy flavour. Various more-or-less deodorized products have been made from it by washing the finished product or by solvent extraction of the starting material. The final product, known as fish protein concentrate, is a light-coloured, tasteless, and odourless powder, but the processing has taken it out of the class of cheap foods. It has been used experimentally to enrich baked goods at the 20 per cent level, but only a limited amount can be added to bread without spoiling the colour, crumb quality, and loaf volume.

As is the case with so many novel foods, fish meal is not new. It was eaten in ancient Rome; according to Apicius fish entrails and small fish (small red mullet, sprats, or anchovy) were salted and dried in the sun and sprinkled on to food as a condiment. Even the idea of using fish meal as an extra protein in baked goods is not very new since biscuits enriched with fish flour were exhibited by the Norwegian Department of Agriculture in 1876.

In recent years several new products have been made from surplus fish, such as fish sausages, crisps, and chips. The fish is minced and mixed with fat, starch, and water. It is dyed and flavoured, and is said to taste like meat sausages. The crisps expand when dropped into hot oil in the same way as savoury crisps made from prawns (prawn crackers), which have been introduced to the British market from the East. Fish chips look like ordinary potato chips, but they are a mixture of a potato and fish—fish and chips all in one. So far none of these products has been exploited commercially in Great Britain.

It would be possible to increase the food potential of the sea if, instead of eating the fish, man made use of the primary food that the fish themselves eat, namely the plankton.

PRIMARY FOODS

Primary foods are those that we eat at first hand (like fruits, vegetables, and cereals), as distinct from secondary foods (like meat, fish, milk, and eggs) that have been produced by the animal who ate the primary food in the first place. The biological chain from plankton to man's food is long and extremely inefficient. It is said that by the time the smallest fish have eaten the plankton, and in turn been eaten by larger fish, and eventually the largest fish have reached the size required by man, 10 000 tonnes of plankton are used to produce a single tonne of fish. On that basis it is theoretically possible to increase the harvest of food from the seas by this enormous factor. Whether the energy cost of sieving vast quantities of sea-water would be reasonable has not been settled. The taste of plankton is said to be similar to that of anchovies.

Another primary food of the sea is krill, small shrimps (*Euphasia superba*) that are the food of whales. This is used in Japan and Thailand, and the potential is said to be 50–100 million tonnes per year. Russia has developed krill fishing in the Antarctic where the shrimps have multiplied enormously in recent years. They are processed on a factory ship where the edible flesh is squeezed out between rollers, cooked, and frozen into compact blocks. The composition is 20–24 per cent protein, 4 per cent fat, 4 per cent minerals, and 70 per cent water, and it has the taste of cooked fresh shrimp. The price in 1970 was $U.S. 2–3 per kg, and it was being sold mixed with cheese.

In terms of energy, food grain yields ten times as much as beef or eggs for the same area of land; and starchy foods (potatoes, cassava, and bananas) yield twenty times as much. Even for protein the plant sources are more efficient in terms of land areas: legumes yield about five to ten times as much as dairy cows (Table 8.1).

TABLE 8.1

Efficiency of production: animal versus vegetable foods

Yields (millions of kilocalories per hectare†)			
Beef	0·4	Grain	5·2
Eggs	0·5	Rice	6·5
Butter	0·8	Potatoes	11·5
Milk	1·8	Cassava	11·8
Bananas	12·4	Sugar	24·7

Land needed in hectares† to produce 20 kg of protein (sufficient for one adult for a year)			
Dairy cows	1·1–2·7	Beans	0·25
Chickens	3·4	Grass	0·25–0·6
Sheep	2·0–4·7	Cereals	0·6
Pigs	5·0	Potatoes	0·7
Beef	2·5–6·0		

† 1 hectare = 2·74 acres.

However, it must be borne in mind that the animals eat
many foods that we would not normally eat, such as grass,
so the increased efficiency would be achieved only if the
grassland were replaced by cultivated crops. What is perhaps
more important is that many people prefer animal foods.

Green leaves

There are, however, several possibilities for obtaining food
from primary sources which could be very profitable. Green
leaves, such as grass, jungle foliage, and cabbage, contain
1·5–5 per cent protein and are plentiful in all parts of the
world. Their high content of indigestible cellulose prevents
us from eating more than a small amount. The problem
has been overcome by separating the protein from the
cellulose, a process first carried out by Rouelle in 1773,
and revived and stimulated in recent time by N. W. Pirie.

The process is quite simple. The green material is
macerated and the juice squeezed out. The fibre residue
still contains some protein as well as fat and starch, and can
be used as cattle feed. The extracted juice is heated to
coagulate the protein, which can be filtered off.

A wide variety of raw materials have been treated in this
way. They include waste from crops like cotton, jute, sugar
beet and cane, sweet potato, bananas, cassava, and peas. With
this process young plants of wheat, barley, and rye can be
cropped several times during the growing season, compared
with the single crop of grain that is now obtained. Grass
also provides a continuing supply of protein. At the same
time there are enormous supplies of plants, such as water
hyacinth and water lettuce, that choke up waterways in some
areas of the world and have to be removed at considerable
cost.

Another important consideration is the efficient use of our
outside source of energy, sunlight. As Pirie has pointed out,
many of our domesticated crops do not make the best use of
the energy supply. We crop our wheat, for example, when
the sunshine is near its maximum and the wheat plant has
gone brown and ceased to photosynthesize. Yields equivalent

to 1–2 tonnes of protein per hectare have been obtained in Great Britain by cropping wheat leaves when they are green. This is 25–50 times as much protein as is obtained on the same area from cereal grains, and 10–20 times as much as that obtained from legumes.

Like so many good ideas there are drawbacks. So far the colour and flavour have not proved acceptable in feeding trials. These trials are continuing, and improvements may be brought about by food technologists or even the cook. But so far leaf protein for human consumption has not caught on.

Oilseeds

Oilseeds such as cotton, sesame, groundnut, and sunflower are crushed for their oil which is used for margarine and cooking oils, and the protein residues have been used for many years in animal feed. They are now being used to a small extent directly in human foods, both in protein-rich weaning foods for babies and to enrich a variety of other foods.

SUBSTITUTE FOODS

Textured foods from soya bean

One of the major developments in novel food is the manufacture of meat analogues or textured vegetable proteins. These are made from soya-bean meal (although other beans can be used) which is processed, textured, and flavoured to resemble meat. They have several advantages. First, as discussed elsewhere, it is relatively wasteful to feed soya to animals and then get the meat second-hand; it is more efficient to eat the soya directly. Secondly, the textured products offer several advantages to the food manufacturer. Products can be made of any shape, colour, flavour, and texture. Unlike meat they are free from gristle and excessive amounts of fat, so there is nothing to be trimmed off and wasted. The product is standardized, and it can even be made to fit the can. Thirdly, these soya products are cheaper than meat.

Nutritionally, the quality of soya protein is not much below that of meat; and other nutrients that we obtain from meat, like vitamins and iron, could be added. It would be possible, by such additions, to make the soya product more nutritious than meat. These meat analogues have been on the market in the United States for several years but have only recently become available in Great Britain. They can be used as foods themselves or mixed with meat in foods like hamburgers, sausages, stews, pizzas, and pies, or mixed with fish in fish cakes. Although most of the research effort has gone into making meat-like foods, the vegetable proteins can also be made to resemble fruit, nuts, and shredded coconut.

There are two types of meat substitute on the market, an extruded product and a more expensive spun product.

The extruded 'meat' is made by mixing soya flour into a dough with water, salt, and flavours. The mixture is heated under pressure and forced through dies, when it suddenly fluffs up and dries to form a spongy mass. This is chopped into pieces and can be stored for many months. When it is wanted it is simply cooked with water, which makes it swell up to three times the dry weight.

Some people believe that the spun product tastes better and has a texture more like that of meat. It is made by spinning fibres of the soya protein rather like artificial silk; in fact, the process uses similar spinnerets. The soya protein is dissolved in alkali to form a viscous solution and is squirted through holes. As the protein solution comes through the holes, it is coagulated in an acid–salt mixture so that it sets in fine, hair-like fibres. These are pressed into blocks, and are flavoured and coloured with the addition of starch, cereals, fat, emulsifiers, and other materials.

By grouping the holes in the spinnerets and altering their arrangement and size, products of varying toughness and shape can be made in order to simulate fish, meat, poultry, shellfish, etc. For example, 'streaky bacon' can be made by colouring groups of fibres white or red and mixing in fat in the right places.

While these products are a monument to the skill of the food technologist, they are not very new. Among the earlier attempts to simulate meat was a patent taken out in 1906 by Dr. John Kellogg, the father of the corn flake, showing how to make a vegetable 'chop' from wheat gluten.

The onlooker might believe that meat substitutes were developed in response to a shortage of food in the developing countries, where meat may be eaten only on festive occasions. On the contrary, the product was developed largely in response to a requirement of the Western food processor for a standardized material and to eke out the meat that was growing scarcer and more costly. It may well find a place in the diets of developing countries, but its manufacture requires a high degree of technology such as is not found in those countries. Nor is the major problem of hunger found among people who buy their food from factories in the big cities but rather among the peasant farmers who grow their own food. Often what is wanted is more food of the usual kind rather than new foods.

Coffee whitener

A substitute food that is perhaps much better known is coffee whitener. Despite the long-established and widespread practice of adding cow's milk to tea and coffee, it was felt desirable to improve the product for reasons of economy, ease of handling, improved shelf-life, and appeal to vegetarians. Synthetic or imitation milk is defined in the United States as a substance made from non-dairy protein and fat ingredients to resemble fluid milk. Fat appears to be the most important ingredient in providing what is termed 'whitening' power and 'body'. In fact, sodium caseinate, obtained from milk, is usually the protein source but according to United States legislation, this is termed a 'non-dairy protein'. Coffee whiteners are greatly inferior to milk as a source of nutrients but are generally used in small amounts as a convenience rather than as a food.

Enriched grain

A substitute food of quite a different calibre and purpose is the imitation cereal grain. This is made to enrich wheat, or rice. One method of improving nutrient intake, when people cannot be persuaded or are unable to improve their eating habits, is to add the required nutrients to the staple food. For example, in many countries, including Great Britain, vitamins of the B complex, iron, and calcium are added to white flour, and vitamins A and D are added to margarine. In some countries iodine is added to salt, and vitamin C is added to fruit juices.

The addition of nutrient mixtures to flour is not as easy as it sounds, since such a small quantity of nutrient has to be added to vast amounts of flour. The vitamins are added at the rate of 1 part of vitamin mixture to 30 million parts of flour, and the calcium carbonate at the rate of 1 part in 300 parts of flour. A bigger problem arises in the developing countries where people buy their wheat unground or where the staple is rice, since the powdered nutrients cannot easily be added to the wheat or rice grains.

One method of enriching rice (which was discussed earlier) is to spray a solution of the nutrients on to the grains and then to coat them with a water-insoluble but digestible protective layer. Wheat is sometimes enriched by soaking the grain in a solution of nutrients and then adding a small amount of the enriched grain to the bulk of the wheat. Another method is to make a mixture of the required additives in high concentration into a shape resembling the grain and to mix a small quantity of the artificial grains with the bulk of the wheat. The artificial grains must look exactly the same as the real ones, otherwise the discerning housewife might pick them out and discard them.

A parallel approach to improving nutrient intake is to make a food that looks like the traditional food, say rice, from raw materials that are more readily available and of higher nutritive value. One of these that was made on a small scale was called synthetic rice or tapioca-macaroni.

It was made from 80–90 parts of tapioca flour, which is available in large amounts but is low in protein, with 10–20 parts of peanut flour, also freely available and rich in protein. The mixture was shaped to resemble grains, and it was even polished to resemble white rice, which was the preferred food.

Caviare

A somewhat more exotic preparation of less nutritional interest is simulated caviare. The pollution of the Caspian Sea—the source of 90 per cent of the world's caviare—has reduced the catch of sturgeon and the valuable by-product caviare, which is sold in Great Britain at £8–12 per 100 g (depending on the variety).

Presumably for domestic consumption, since a simulated product would scarcely sell elsewhere, the Russians started to make synthetic caviare on a pilot-plant scale in 1963. It is made from any soluble protein such as egg white, casein, or isolated protein. The solution is squirted through fine needles into hot oil where surface tension causes it to break up into beads of the required size. At the same time, the hot oil coagulates the protein. The beads settle to the bottom of the vessel and are collected, dyed black, salted, and flavoured.

PROTEIN FROM MICRO-ORGANISMS

The other area of excitement in the field of 'new foods' is factory production of micro-organisms, such as yeasts, bacteria, algae, and moulds. All these are rich in protein. Bacteria contain 47–87 per cent of the dry weight as protein, yeast 50 per cent, fungi 40 per cent, and algae 40 per cent. The potential yield, mostly by extrapolation from small-scale production, is quite fantastic. For example, in one day

a 1000-kg steer will produce 1 kg protein,
1000 kg of soya beans will produce 86 kg protein,
1000 kg of yeast will produce 4000 kg protein, and

1000 kg of bacteria could produce 10 million kg of protein!

Another advantage of this method of protein production, since we have limited land available for farming, is the limited space needed: a hectare of land will produce 10 kg of protein as meat, 17 kg as milk, 80 kg as peanuts, 110 kg as grass, or 2600 kg as algae. It has been calculated that the entire protein needs of the world could be grown in a volume of 10^{13} litres, if algae were used as a source.

The micro-organisms fall into two groups, those that need to be provided with a source of energy (the moulds, yeasts, and bacteria) and those that can use the energy of the sunshine in photosynthesis (the algae). The latter need be supplied only with carbon dioxide, mineral salts, and nitrogen, and some varieties can even make use of atmospheric nitrogen.

The energy sources for the moulds, yeasts, and bacteria is carbohydrate, which could come from, for example, starch by-products, molasses from sugar refining, waste from fruit canning, sulphite liquors from paper-pulp manufacture, and hydrocarbons in the form of petroleum by-products and natural gas. This group of micro-organisms can also be grown on animal waste and domestic waste.

Yeast

Molasses is a waste product in sugar refining, apart from its considerable value in fermenting to rum. During the Second World War it was used as a raw material for the production of yeast with the intention of supplementing the protein supplies. Unfortunately it never became accepted because of its strong flavour. The idea was later revived—this time for animal feed—using petroleum by-products as a source of energy. Hundreds of thousands of tonnes of yeast are now being produced as a protein supplement for pigs and poultry. It serves as a replacement for soya-bean meal and fish meal which are often in short supply.

Bacteria as food

A new potential source of food followed the discovery, in 1959, that bacteria proliferated in the waxes that accumulate during oil refining. The de-waxing of petroleum materials by bacteria resulted in the formation of a large quantity of bacterial protein.

The original purpose of the research had been to recover the petroleum, since the bacteria selectively consume the paraffins leaving behind the de-waxed gas oil that the refiner wants, but both products have a value. It has been found that 10 tonnes of basic gas oil can be de-waxed to produce 9 tonnes of refined gas oil and 1 tonne of bacterial protein. Generally, phosphate and nitrate must be added, but in 1964 an organism was isolated which would oxidize methane to supply its energy and take its nitrogen for protein synthesis from the atmosphere. Methane is a useful raw material since it is found in extremely large quantities lying over oil-fields (as in the deposits of North Sea gas), and in the major oil-fields of the Middle East, 50–100 million tonnes of methane go to waste each year.

Bacterial protein is not at present intended for human consumption but for animal feed. The research is not in so advanced a stage as that on yeast, which underwent more than 20 years of feeding trials before it went on sale in 1972, but bacterial protein has enormous potential.

Fungi

Mushrooms—which are fungi—are grown as a raw material for the food industry. In Brazil the ordinary mushroom, *Agaricus campestris*, is grown on molasses; it is said that the residue from the local brandy manufacture is sufficient to produce 90 000 tonnes of mycelium annually. Morel mushrooms are also grown on a commercial scale but are used as a flavouring rather than a food. The fungus of current interest is the mould *Fusarium*, which is being produced in a pilot plant in the Lord Rank Research Laboratories in Great Britain. It is grown on waste starch and has the particular advantage that the mould filaments already have a structure, whereas all the other materials are powders that would have to be textured to be made into an acceptable human food.

Algae

Algae obtain their energy from sunlight. Some forms, such as seaweeds, are already a significant part of the diet in Japan.

There are several pilot plants in different parts of the world producing unicellular algae (*Chlorella* and *Scenedesmus*) economically. Compared with conventional crops there are no useless twigs, leaves, and roots, the whole plant can be eaten, and the yield is much higher. For example, 50 times as much protein can be obtained from algae as from wheat or maize grown on the same area. What is even more attractive from the production point of view is that the process is continuous and can be automated.

The algae make very efficient use of the energy of sunshine compared with higher plants. Sunlight radiates about 17 500 million kilocalories per hectare of ground, but plants convert only 0·05–0·25 per cent of this into edible material. Part of the time during the growth of the plant the sun shines on bare soil. Even after the seeds have sprouted, energy is wasted on the empty spaces between the plants. Only when they are large enough to cover the soil is the energy being reasonably well used, and even then the arrangement of the leaves is often far from perfect for maximum efficiency. Algae can grow in large tanks and convert 2·5 per cent of the energy of the sun into edible material, which makes them 10–50 times as efficient as conventional crops. *Chlorella* can produce 100 tonnes of dry matter per hectare per year compared with just over 1 tonne from soya beans.

As recently as 1962 tribes living around Lake Chad in Northern Africa were observed skimming blue–green algae,

Spirulina, from the surface of the lake to use as a food. It was subsequently found that the Aztecs near Mexico City had been doing the same since early times. Not only is *Spirulina* already accepted as a food (by some people) but it has the added virtue that it uses nitrogen from the atmosphere. However, there is still a long way to go before algae are economically, nutritionally, and gastromically a success.

Of the four types of organisms under investigation, yeast and bacteria are intended for animal feeds, while algae and fungi are intended for human foods. However, health authorities have to be satisfied that they are safe to eat. The problem is that because the cells grow so rapidly they contain relatively large amounts of nucleoproteins which in the body form uric acid, the substance that causes gout. They also contain a variety of unusual substances in the cell wall, and it is not known if we can tolerate these materials if they are eaten in the amounts that would be involved in a food.

FOOD FROM NON-FOOD SOURCES

Two examples are of interest, carbohydrate from wood and protein from wool.

Large amounts of wood are wasted in timber mills. The figure for the United States has been estimated at 40 million tonnes annually, together with about 5 million tonnes of carbohydrate wasted in paper manufacture. Wood is mostly hemicellulose, which is not digested even by ruminants, but is very easily hydrolysed with acid. This is not a new process: it dates back over a hundred years and was used commercially in the production of spirits in the United States until 1913. The wood was hydrolysed to glucose and this was fermented to alcohol at the rate of some 22 000 litres a day until the process was ousted by cheap molasses. Hydrolysed wood was also used in Germany in the Second World War.

Wool, containing 60 per cent protein, at one time sold at the same price as meat, which contains only 10–15 per cent protein, and the lower grades of wool were even cheaper than meat. The protein in wool cannot be digested (except by the larva of the clothes moth), but methods of making it soluble have been investigated in New Zealand. It has been added to baked products, replacing 40 per cent of the cereal, and found to be acceptable, but the nutritional value has not yet been thoroughly examined. A similar product is acid-hydrolysed hog bristle, prepared by a method patented in Germany. Its suggested use is as a meat-flavoured base for soups and stock cubes.

SYNTHETIC FOODS

It is often asked whether, one day, our food will be synthesized. Although we can already synthesize many of our food-stuffs, the answer is 'no'. This is because it is far more efficient, and will become increasingly so as fossil fuels become more expensive (if they are even available), to grow crops in the old-fashioned way using the free energy of sunshine. The vast scale of production from millions of square kilometres of soil could not be imagined as a factory process. In any case, the materials synthesized would still have to be fashioned into steaks, fruits, vegetables, and all the other delightful textures that people like.

Some of the raw materials of food manufacture are already synthetic, such as all the vitamins and many of the flavours, colours, and texturizing substances. It is possible to synthesize fats and carbohydrates, but the processes are not to be compared, at present, with crop cultivation.

Fat is the only major foodstuff that has been synthesized on an industrial scale. Its synthesis from petroleum paraffins was first developed in 1884 in Germany and was seriously investigated there during the First World War. When natural fats became available again, interest waned, to be revived again during the Second World War.

Synthetic fats differ from natural ones in that they

contain both odd- and even-numbered chains of carbon atoms, whereas natural fats contain only even-numbered chains. When they are eaten, part of the odd-numbered chains are excreted in the urine as dicarboxylic acids. In addition, synthetic fats contain various branched chains and other modifications which give rise to abnormal excretory products in the urine. Nevertheless, 100 000 tonnes of synthetic fats were consumed in Germany in the 1940s.

Today, with a greater knowledge of food toxicology, it is doubtful whether we would want to consume a product so different from ordinary fat. However, with adequate economic stimulus a satisfactory product (including, if necessary, the various phospholipids and lipoproteins that are found in natural occurring fats) could probably be synthesized. At present, it is far cheaper to grow oil seeds.

Organic chemists synthesized glucose and fructose in the last century. The double sugar, sucrose, and the more complex carbohydrate, starch, have been synthesized in the laboratory with the aid of enzyme systems, but only in small amounts, and the process cannot be regarded as a practical proposition.

All the amino acids are available in synthetic form, but only lysine and methionine are cheap. These two are the ones that are usually in shortest supply in protein foods; they are added to some animal feeds when they are cheaper than the corresponding amount of extra protein. Animal feeds can be exactly priced, and the advantage of reducing the quantity and quality of protein and making this up with the added synthetic amino acids can be assessed precisely. We cannot be so precise with human feeding, so it is not clear whether there is any advantage in supplementing human foods with amino acids, although it is done to a limited extent.

Some degree of success has been achieved in the laboratory synthesis of proteins. Long-chain polypeptides were synthesized early in the twentieth century by the laborious method of linking amino acids one by one. More recently in the 1960s protein-like materials have been made by treating mixtures of amino acids with electrical discharges or with heat, but the material cannot be regarded in any way as a foodstuff.

RECENT PROGRESS

The growing demand for food emphasizes the need to explore the potential of every one of the methods proposed, whether they are extensions of conventional methods or entirely new. The potential of the novel foods is enormous; but so far as we can see, in the future the greater part of our needs will be supplied by conventional foods, preferably bigger, better, tastier, and more convenient.

In the Western world the increasing demand for food over the past few years has coincided with rapid developments in food technology, and increasing affluence has allowed people to pay for variations on the basic themes. Food production in large centres of population has followed the modern approach to mass production in large engineering complexes instead of in smaller, family businesses. In Great Britain thousands of small bakers have been replaced by massive, automatic bakeries producing millions of loaves a week. This has been going on for many years and is the inevitable result of modern industrial practice.

Such changes have altered some of our eating habits. Foods that were somewhat rare because they were expensive have become cheap and commonplace. The best example, perhaps, is the chicken: in the 1930s it was a rare treat for most families, more expensive than meat and fish. The developments that took place in the 1950s exemplify the range of scientific advances involved. First came the idea of large-scale production instead of small flocks of birds. Then the economist-nutritionist pointed out that the stage of rapid growth, which is when the farmer gets a good return on chicken flesh for the least expenditure of food, is over in the early weeks. After that the bird grows more slowly, so that the rate of production of flesh per unit of food eaten falls. Hence the arrival of the broiler chicken, ready to eat after about 10 weeks instead of 20 weeks, more economical to produce and therefore cheaper.

The geneticists then produced a bird that gave the most efficient yield under these conditions and the nutritionist developed the optimum diet for the bird. Large-scale production for efficient utilization of plant and machinery meant the application of engineering principles to slaughter, plucking and cleaning. The development of plastic-film wrapping provided protection during transport and visibility during sale; hygiene was an absolute essential. The end-result is that not only did two chickens grow where one grew before, but that the production of chickens went up from 25 million in 1956 to 330 million in 1973.

FUTURE DEVELOPMENTS

The type of development now going on in the food industry is demonstrated on a single page of a recent copy of *Food Processing Industry*, a monthly trade magazine. The following developments are discussed: Findus Ltd. is to market the traditional Italian dish, lasagne, aimed at the working wives; Chambourcy Dairy Products Ltd. is adding grapefruit to its range of yogurts; Irish Biscuits Ltd. is adding coconut mallows to its list; Hofels Pure Foods Ltd. is marketing yogurt in tablet and freeze-dried powder form; Country Kitchen Foods Ltd. plan to establish for the first time a national brand of fresh mushrooms.

If these developments have already taken place, what can happen in the future? It has already been reported that square tomatoes and apples are on their way—they would be easier to pack, of course. Square fruits have been produced by boxing them during growth, but genetic manipulation is the objective. Geneticists have already succeeded in producing plants with high yield, eye appeal, uniformity of ripening time to aid harvesting, uniformity of appearance to aid packaging and sales, resistance to disease, and mechanical strength to allow them to stand up to harvesting by machine and to withstand the rigours of travel.

Celery has a habit of 'bolting', so non-bolting varieties are available. For the housewife who likes her broccoli to stay green after cooking, the geneticist crossed white cauliflower with broccoli. For those who like their cauliflower white, there is a variety that curls its leaves over the flower to protect it from the sun. Seedless tomatoes were produced years ago by hormone treatment, but consumers seemed not to like them. On the other hand, seedless cucumbers may soon be available, with the added attraction that they do not need peeling.

Sometimes it is the manufacturer who has to be satisfied rather than the housewife. The user has to decide whether he wants the farmer to supply high-protein barley for feeding animals or low-protein barley for making beer. Even the hamburger seller has his special requirements—large onion rings—and these, too, are on the way.

Sometimes the breeder leaves the job to the food technologist. For example, a long egg is needed to fill a meat-and-egg pie; otherwise what does the shopkeeper do with the end pieces without egg, which no one wants? The manufacturer requires an egg that is long enough to fill the whole length of his pie and that will give every customer his share of the yolk as well as the white. So the technologist produced long cylindrical eggs several feet long, made from ordinary eggs. The British patent was taken out in 1973 by a French group. It illustrates the basic science behind what might appear to be a trivial objective. 'The apparatus consists of three hoppers to receive the yolk, white, and filler respectively. The white is pumped into the outer annular space between concentric pipes leading from the hoppers and cooked by an external jacket. The yolk is pumped into the inner annular space and cooked electromagnetically between electrodes. The filling occupies the centre space. The "endless tubular hard-boiled egg" is plastic-wrapped as it leaves the apparatus.'

Parallel developments include leafless peas, long-stalked blackcurrants, marble-sized potatoes, half-metre apple 'trees' producing fruit on a single stem. For the scientists there seems to be no limit. Only one thing is certain: we cannot feed man with a pill unless it weighs 700 g, since this is the minimum weight of the basic materials needed to supply his energy needs and nutrients.

9

Getting our money's worth

In the middle of the last century a sweet manufacturer in Bradford attempted to swindle his customers by adulterating his sweets with plaster of Paris. Unfortunately the chemist who supplied him gave him white arsenic by mistake, and 15 people died.

We are entitled to ask for both honesty and safety in our foods, and nowadays we get both, but pure-food laws have been with us only since 1860. Before that people often did not get what they paid for, and food was frequently adulterated for profit. Even in ancient Rome, bakers were accused of adding 'white earth' to their bread. Adulterated foods may have been usually harmless, but they were also sometimes fatal. The only protection for the public was the system of Assizes that controlled the price and quality of bread and ale. In the days of King John a baker found guilty of selling mouldy bread was paraded round the town on a dung cart. However, in 1820 the public conscience was stirred a little by the publication of the first chemical analysis of food by Professor Frederick Accum. It summarized 20 years of investigation, and revealed the widespread adulteration of many common foods.

Accum found that, since the public liked matured beer, some brewers and publicans simulated the storage period by adding sulphuric acid to it. If the beer was kept too long and went sour, it was neutralized with powdered oyster shells. Watered beer had no 'head', so iron sulphate was added; watered gin had no 'bite', so sulphuric acid was added.

Bean meal, slaked lime, and alum were put into bread; sour wine was sweetened with sugar of lead; and spices were diluted with flour. Other swindling included inserting pieces of iron in a loaf of bread and putting sand and husks into other food. At a time when only 2·7 million kg of genuine tea was being imported, another 1·8 million kg was being made from the leaves of ash, aloe, and elder collected from the British countryside and coloured on copper plates. The first chemical analysis, in the nineteenth century, showed that sulphuric acid was being sold as vinegar.

Other dangers to health included innocent attempts to make foods more attractive. Foods were coloured with salts of arsenic, lead, and mercury; the rind of Gloucester cheese was coloured with vermillion (mercuric sulphide) and red lead; and nearly all sweets were coloured with lead chromate, vermillion, copper, arsenate, white lead, or organboge.

In Great Britain, the adulteration of food was increasingly practised in the larger cities during the nineteenth century. The population was increasing rapidly, against a background of inadequate sanitation, poor water supplies, and crowded housing conditions. The rapidly increasing demand for food led to easy profits, and there were no laws to protect the consumers.

The same situation existed in other countries. In Canada the first food analysis, carried out in 1877, showed that half the samples tested were adulterated. Cheaper grades of tea contained used leaves; coffee contained roasted wheat, peas, and beans; butter contained lard and excess water. In the United States, where there was widespread adulteration of commercial syrups, glucose was found in honey, cane molasses, and maple syrup.

Even though the adulteration of food had been 'unmasked' in 1820, nothing was done about it, and adulteration is believed to have increased in Great Britain towards the middle of the nineteenth century. However, other chemists continued Accum's work, and they showed that flour often contained potato flour, pipeclay, and powdered flints.

In the 1840s there were known to be eight factories in London whose output consisted of used tea leaves. According to a report of the Chemical Department of the Inland Revenue, persons were employed to buy up exhausted leaves at hotels, coffee-houses, and other places at 2½d. to 3d. (1–1½p) per pound (about ½ kg). These were taken to the factory, mixed with a solution of gum and re-dried. After this the dried leaves, if for black tea, were mixed with rose-pink and black lead to 'face' them, as it is termed in the trade. Other colouring materials included Prussian blue, turmeric, copper carbonate, and lead chromate (the last two are poisonous). There were also 'bread doctors' and 'brewers' druggists'—business consultants of the day who helped packers and manufacturers to adulterate their products effectively. Coffee was simply adulterated with chicory, and a patent was taken out in Liverpool in 1851 for a machine that compressed chicory into the shape of coffee beans.

The public conscience was eventually stirred into action when in 1851 the editor of *Lancet* began to publish a series of weekly articles reporting the results of the analyses of named foods. The first general pure-food laws to exist in any country were passed by the Parliament of Great Britain in 1860. There have been various amending Acts, notably those of 1938 and 1955 (the Foods and Drugs Act).

The new laws were designed to prevent adulteration, improve hygiene, and make food safer. In 1872 Public Analysts were appointed to make sure that the law was obeyed, and it rapidly became effective. In 1877, 19 per cent of all samples analysed were adulterated, but in 1900 only 9 per cent were. In the United States similar developments took place rather later; analysis was put on an official footing by the U.S. Department of Agriculture at the end of the nineteenth century.

The British Food and Drugs Act of 1955 summarizes the present attitude to adulteration. This Act forbids false or misleading descriptions of food, and ensures that the food

is pure and wholesome. It imposes criminal sanctions if
the food is 'not of the nature, or not of the substance, or not
of the quality' demanded by the purchasers. If food is not
of the correct *nature* a variety of food has been supplied
that is different from the one demanded; 'not of the *substance*' means that an incorrect ingredient or adulteration
is present; and the *quality* is determined in the many regulations that specify the composition and ingredients of a
manufactured food. In Great Britain, for example, the
composition of ice-cream, margarine, fruit drinks, jam, and
coffee essences is regulated, and in these instances no list
of ingredients is required on the label. For other foods, the
law demands that the label carries a list of ingredients in
descending order of quantity; for example, manufacturers
are prevented from labelling a product 'cheese and macaroni' if the major ingredient is macaroni. The Food and
Drugs Act prohibits any processing of, additions to, ab-
stractions from, or mixtures with food intended for
consumption that would render it injurious to health. The
Act also gives powers to the Ministers of Health and
Agriculture to make regulations controlling the composition
of food, processing additives, labelling, advertising, and
hygiene.

Adulteration for the purposes of fraud has long since
been done away with in the United States and Great Britain,
and nowadays the Public Analyst has rather different things
to watch for. His work is aimed at preventing accidental
contamination from substances like pesticide residues, dirt,
and pieces of string, making sure that manufactured foods
contain the right amount of the right ingredients, and
making sure that only the permitted chemical additives
are used.

The Public Analyst examines foods that are bought in
the ordinary way, in order to see that the pure-food regulations and laws are obeyed. Moreover, any consumer, if
he has reason to be dissatisfied with what he has bought,
can take the food to the Town Hall, where the Medical
Officer of Health, the Weights and Measures Inspector, or
the Public Analyst will take the necessary action. This

also covers any misleading claims: slimming foods and 'health' foods, as well as all the mundane everyday foods, must not be advertised in a manner likely to mislead the customer, nor can they contain any substance that may be harmful or any colour or preservative that is not specifically permitted by law. There are often infringements of the law; a few are deliberate, although many are accidental— but the manufacturer or retailer is still taken to court and fined. Some of the claims brought to the attention of the Public Analyst are as exotic as they are nonsensical, for example, the cheese described as 'exaltation of Elizabethan flowers cheese' (and said to be made from the milk of cows that had been fed on 'exaltation of Elizabethan flowers'), or beetroot juice, sold as being good for the blood—simply because it was red! The Public Analyst continues to act as guardian of the health of the consumer. At the same time, nowadays he also ensures that all imported foods comply with British law.

The appointment of Public Analysts prompted food manufacturers to employ qualified chemists of their own in their factories. At first the work of the chemists was simply to safeguard their products so that there was no contravention of the law. Later they began to supervise the quality of the products leaving the factories—their appearance, taste, chemical composition, nutritive value, and storage properties.

However, we should not be too complacent or confident that all is now well with our food as is shown by the following recent extract from the *Daily Mail*, 30 April 1974: 'Early this year a scandal broke exposing three major wine producers in Corsica as frauds. They were making red vintages of sulphuric acid, glycerine and colouring. Hundreds of thousands of bottles were involved.'

World food problems

In Great Britain, the United States, and most countries of the Western world there is no shortage of food. Shops and warehouses are full all year round, and fresh fruits and vegetables know no seasons. We can even have fresh strawberries or French beans at any time (at a price), because production in tropical countries and air transport have been organized for this specific purpose.

However, this situation is of very recent origin, and even the more mundane foods have not been with us in such profusion and with such regularity for very long. Our parents will certainly remember that a much smaller variety of food was available before 1950, and that there were temporary shortages (a situation to which we may now be returning!). Our grandparents will remember how food was scarcer at certain times of the year—and their parents would even remember times of famine.

Over man's history there have always been years of plenty and years of famine. Famine and hunger are frequently mentioned in the Old Testament and in contemporary histories of the Middle Ages. Between the beginning of the Christian era and the seventeenth century there was a famine in Europe one year in every five. The droughts, the floods, and the catastrophes that seem to occur so frequently in 'other' countries, especially in the Middle and Far East, are nothing new, and hand in hand with these periodic disasters goes the chronic problem of food shortage.

If the overall problem is summed up by saying 'there is not enough food in the world for the people of the world', then one must add 'and there never has been'. This is possibly an oversimplification, since some people believe that there is enough food in total but that the distribution is faulty. What is new is that the knowledge needed to solve the problem of feeding the world's millions now exists, and there is also a partial willingness of some of the 'haves' to share what they have with the 'have-nots'.

In the Western world chronic shortages of food have been mostly overcome by the use of technology. More food is produced more efficiently; less is lost and wasted. Foods can be processed, preserved, and stored almost indefinitely, and food can be transported easily from any part of the world. The difficulty lies in applying those sophisticated remedies to the developing countries.

The sheer size of the problem is difficult to appreciate. Shipments of surpluses across national boundaries, even where resources are available, make only a minute contribution towards solving the problems of the starving peoples in Africa and the Far East. Most food is eaten in the country in which it is grown. The massive United States aid, under what was termed Public Law 480, made available nearly 10 million tonnes of cereals to developing countries, but this amounted to only 3 per cent of their total energy supply. There was an enormous scheme for the production of groundnuts in East Africa after 1945 in order to supply oil for magarine, and also protein. The scheme did not succeed, and it cost £35 million (in those days). Had it succeeded, a scheme even of that size would have produced only enough peanut oil to replace the deficit resulting from lower exports of peanut oil from India alone.

It is not known exactly how many people are short of food. First, those in need of help fall into two categories: the undernourished and the malnourished. The undernourished are those who do not receive enough food—they are hungry. The malnourished may receive enough food, but it is lacking in one or more nutrients. Secondly, figures are not all that accurate. Official figures indicate that about

300–500 million people are undernourished, and about 1000 million are malnourished, but statistics are difficult to collect. Moreover, the criteria of adequacy are far from precise.

POVERTY, IGNORANCE, AND ILL-HEALTH

Food problems cannot be considered in isolation. They are only one part of the problem facing developing countries, and in those areas a shortage of food is invariably associated with poverty, ignorance, and ill-health.

Poverty includes both low personal incomes, sometimes as low as one-tenth or one-fiftieth of those we are accustomed to in the West, and low State incomes, which means that overall national development is limited and slow. It also means that welfare schemes like school meals, mother–child clinics, or the enrichment of staple foods cannot be afforded, however necessary they may be.

Ignorance stems from the fact that some children receive no schooling at all, many receive only a short elementary education, and only a handful are educated beyond this stage. Clearly this limits the extent to which a community can develop technically and can become industrialized.

Ill-health is a summation of chronic disease, chronic infections, and infestations affecting almost the whole community. Infant and child mortality in underdeveloped countries can be up to 40 times the Western figure, and the expectation of life is only half that of the Western nations.

None of these factors can be considered in isolation. Malnutrition and infection go hand in hand, the one causes and aggravates the other. Poverty limits not only the family's ability to purchase foods but its ability to purchase medicines, and can militate against education of children. Poverty on a national scale limits the imports of food, medical services, and education; ignorance hinders progress in solving all these problems.

POPULATION GROWTH

An overriding factor in the problem of world nutrition is the recent rapid increase in population. While enormous efforts have been partially successful in increasing the overall food production year by year, the increasing number of mouths to feed has ensured that there is no more food available per head of the world's population as a whole than there was in 1939—before the Food and Agriculture Organization and World Health Organization were established. Vast schemes of irrigation and land reclamation, such as the Aswan High Dam in Egypt, have certainly resulted in an increase in the amount of food available, but by the time such schemes are completed, they have often only just kept pace with the increase in population. The Food and Agriculture Organization of the United Nations has estimated that by 1985 the food demand in the developing countries will be nearly $2\frac{1}{2}$ times that of 1962. Two-thirds of this extra demand will have been created by population growth, and only the remaining one-third from the higher consumption of food per person as incomes rise.

The fertility of mankind has not changed over the centuries, but until recently infant mortality was much higher, so that for a thousand years or more the population of the world remained constant. The improvements in the general environment, health services, food supplies, housing conditions, and sanitation, during the last hundred years in the West, have slowly at first then rapidly lowered the numbers of deaths in infancy, so that the population has grown very rapidly.

Between 1650 and 1850 in the world as a whole, the population doubled, after having been practically constant for centuries. The population doubled again in the 80 years up to 1930, and again in the 45 years up to 1975. In Great Britain alone the population increased from 9 million in 1800 to 40 million in 1900. The world population is expected to double again in about 25 years. Hence the term population explosion.

In Britain the improvement of social conditions, which started in the nineteenth century, continued into the twentieth century: there were major medical discoveries and improvements in sanitation; water was chlorinated and milk was pasteurized. The infant mortality rate continued to fall, but the population did not increase as fast as in the previous century since people were now able to control the size of their families. The 40 million people of 1900 grew to 'only' 60 million in 1970. However, this reduction in population size has happened only in the West (although even there a larger family size has recently become popular again in some countries). In the developing countries the general improvements in living standards have led to a fall in the death rate while the birth rate remains high, so that the numbers in these countries are increasing very rapidly. In the developed nations of the West the population doubles (at the present rate) in about 70 years; in a country like Mexico it doubles in 15 years.

The total world population of 3000 million in 1960 was divided into 850 million people in the rich countries and 2100 million in the poor countries. By the end of the century the total population of 6000 million will be made up of 1270 million in the rich countries and 4700 million in the poorer ones. If such figures are difficult to grasp, think of a new Great Britain (in terms of population), being created in the world every 6 months, and think of the housing, drainage, water supplies, schools, transport, welfare, entertainment—and food—needed for those 50 million new people.

WHY SOME PEOPLE DO NOT GET ENOUGH TO EAT

Many people in the world are relatively short of food. There are many reasons for this, including inadequate food production, lack of water, disease, the influence of tradition, and lack of the required technology.

Inadequate production

The most obvious reason for a shortage of food is inadequate production and this, in turn, may be due to shortage of land, poor soil, poor seeds, disease, poor husbandry, or lack of water.

In some areas the peasant farmer has too little land to support his family at an adequate nutritional level. Problems of this kind may call for legal, political, and economic solutions. Improvements in land distribution and land tenure have led to considerable increases in food production in some countries. However, poor soil is not so easy to remedy. Fertilizers are not only relatively costly in the eyes of a peasant farmer but depend on the establishment of a large-scale chemical industry. Similarly, a lack of water may be remedied on a small scale by, for example, bullock-powered irrigation, but on a larger scale irrigation calls for diesel or electric pumps, and on a very large scale it requires great dams and is associated with large-scale development.

Poor husbandry might appear to be the easiest of the problems to tackle, but the gap between having the knowledge and applying it is enormous. It has been said that world food problems could be solved in a season if all the farmers of the world became as efficient as the farmers of Great Britain. We already know how to feed the world properly, but actually doing it presents a gigantic problem. Poor husbandry includes losses from pests and weeds, and the areas where the problem of food shortage is most acute, such as the tropics, are those where the climate promotes the fast growth of these competitors for man's food.

In many countries, after experiencing all the hazards of drought, cold, and storm, after watering and fertilizing, after losing a large proportion of the crops to pests and disease, and after the labour of harvesting, the farmer may lose another third of the crop in store. Inadequate supplies of food may also result from a lack of foreign currency, which is needed for importing seeds, fertilizers, or foodstuffs, or from excessive zeal in exporting cash crops instead of growing food for local consumption.

Unbalanced diets

Apart from actual food shortages, much suffering is caused by the lack of nutrients in an otherwise adequate diet. For example, a diet may supply adequate energy and protein, but if it is deficient in vitamin B1, beri-beri will result, and if it is deficient in niacin, pellagra will follow. Similarly there may be a mineral deficiency, and in some groups of the population (such as infants), there may be a relative shortage of protein.

This problem of unbalanced diets usually arises when there is heavy dependence on single foods. In some areas 60 per cent, or even 70 or 80 per cent, of the total food supply comes from one single foodstuff. If this is a 'good' food, such as wheat, there may be no malnutrition, but if the staple food is lacking in a nutrient then disease will be widespread.

Deficiency disease is almost a national heritage in some areas. If the staple food (which becomes the staple for reasons of climate, convenience, or tradition), is maize, which lacks available niacin (and is short of the amino acid tryptophan which can be converted into niacin), then pellagra will be endemic in the population. If it is national habit to polish brown rice and remove the germ with the husk, then beri-beri will be endemic. The Indians in Hyderabad are virtually condemned to pellagra because their staple food is a millet (jowar) that lacks niacin and contains an imbalance of amino acids that precipitates the disease. Children in the same area are condemned to vitamin A deficiency because they eat so few foods that supply the vitamin. In some areas, where availability and national taste permit, red palm oil is used for cooking, making vitamin A deficiency virtually impossible; yet only a few kilometres away, if this oil is not used, the deficiency may be quite common. If the staple food is cassava, plantain, or yam (which are low in protein), then the diet as a whole is likely to be poor in protein.

Because of the poor quality of the staple foods, pellagra occurs periodically in parts of Africa, the Middle East, and

Latin America; beri-beri occurs in the Far East and the Pacific area; vitamin A deficiency occurs in parts of Africa, Asia, and Latin America; while anaemia, goitre, and kwashiorkor (protein-energy malnutrition in children) are widespread. It is only when the diet is as mixed as it is in the Western world that single foods have little overall effect on the quality of the diet. We can, of course, eat polished rice with impunity since it is only a small part of our diet and we obtain vitamin B1 from many other foods, but this same rice can cause death in some parts of the world simply because it is so large a proportion of the diet.

It is sometimes said that there would be enough food for everyone if it were properly distributed. National balance sheets are compiled by adding imports to the food produced, subtracting exports, losses, stockpiling, and seeds, and finally dividing the total available food by the total population. However, even if this figure is well above the nutritional needs of the average individual, there can still be malnutrition or undernutrition because of the inequality of distribution. There may be poor distribution within any one country, for reasons of geography, lack of money, or family habits.

Geographically, people living near a river or lake or the sea will have access to fish, which are not available to those living further away, particularly when there is limited transport and no means of preserving the fish. The climate in one part of the country may suit the better foods such as cereals and beans, while another area has a climate that enables only poorer foods like cassava or plantains to flourish. Transport problems may prevent people in the mountains or remote villages from getting adequate supplies.

The economic reasons for poor distribution are obvious, but problems are also caused by the unequal distribution within the family. In many places it is the custom to serve the father first, so that he gets the most and the best. The sons may come next in the order of feeding, and the mother may be low on the list, despite her nutritional needs during pregnancy and nursing. The baby, the member of the family with the greatest proportional needs, usually comes last of all.

Disease

Even when food and the money to buy it are available, malnutrition can arise as a result of disease. Infection and parasitic infestation can lead to the poor absorption of food by the body, and some diseases increase the nutritional needs. Repeated attacks of diarrhoea and vomiting can cause serious malnutrition. The commonest cause of iron-deficiency anaemia is hookworm infestation. Many diseases, especially fevers, cause losses of nutrients from the body, so that during convalescence there is a greatly increased need for nutrients. Where food supplies are barely adequate to satisfy the demands of a healthy individual, frequent disease may mean nutritional disaster.

The influence of tradition

It is recognized that man is a most illogical creature when it comes to his eating habits. The Englishman hangs pheasant for a fortnight before eating it but would regard chicken as bad if kept as long. He will not eat dog, horse, frogs, or snails, which other people quite enjoy. Since there is a large variety of food available in Great Britain, such idiosyncrasies have no effect on the nutritional status of anyone, but when foods are very limited such prejudices can be harmful.

Many foods are refused for traditional, cultural, or religious reasons. Many such taboos apply to babies and expectant mothers, and deprive them of foods that they need. A woman living on the borderline of an adequate diet needs extra protein during pregnancy but may be prohibited from eating fish for fear that the child will be born with scales. Chicken may be banned to children in the belief that their hands will become shaky; meat, eggs, or fish, or sometimes all three, may be withheld from children for a variety of reasons.

People will go to great lengths to obtain the food they want, even so far as refusing what is available. In Northern Nigeria the staple foods are the cereals sorghum, millet, and maize. Ibos and Yorubas from East and West Nigeria living in the North will go hungry rather than consume this local diet, and cassava flour (gari) has to be brought from hundreds of kilometres away. In fact the cereal diet is far more nutritious, but to these people that is not a convincing argument when it is weighed against their likes and dislikes.

Poor technology

If advances in technology have been mainly responsible for the abolition of food shortages in the Western world, then lack of technology is partly responsible for the continuing shortages in the developing countries. Apart from the technology of food production, the lack of knowledge of food processing means that seasonal surpluses are wasted and that people live well only immediately after the harvest.

CONCLUSION

It is clear from the multiplicity of factors involved that the problem of feeding the peoples of the world is vast and complex, and it calls for the application of many disciplines and sciences besides nutrition.

One problem that faces mankind in the long term is the availability of living space. It has an allied question: 'How many people can the earth supply with food?' At present it is estimated that only half the arable land is in use. Of course, farming can be made more efficient, but it is estimated that a minimum of 2 hectares of land is needed to support 5 people. By extrapolation (a dangerous occupation), it has been calculated that we will reach this amount of arable land per head sometime between the year 2000 and 2050. It has also been calculated that if all the land now under cultivation were as productive as the farms of Holland, the world could support 60 000 million people on a typically Dutch diet. Judging from the past, the improvements in productivity such as that just mentioned seem extremely unlikely. However, the figure does emphasize how difficult it is to guess when the earth, even with the land under the most productive cultivation, will no longer be able to feed its population.

Developments in the production of novel foods on the factory scale underline this. It takes 2 hectares of land to feed 5 people, but microscopic green algae grown in tanks can supply the energy and protein needs of these 5 people in only 5 square metres of space. It is calculated, no doubt by extrapolation from very small-scale production, that it would need only (!) 10^{13} litres of bacterial biomass to provide the entire world with its protein requirements.

While we can make our calculations for the future we must not forget that we are no longer thinking of the distant future but possibly of a time only a single generation away. We must also bear in mind that Malthus's original calculation still holds true, namely that population multiplies at a geometric rate, while food supplies (at least conventionally produced) multiply arithmetically.

Suggestions for further reading

P. FISHER and A. E. BENDER (1975). *The value of food* (2nd edn) (Oxford University Press) is an elementary textbook on nutrition.

Individual topics are dealt with in the Value of Food Series; titles include:

S. H. CAKEBREAD (1975). *Sugar and chocolate confectionery.*
J. SCADE (1975). *Cereals.*
J. W. G. PORTER (1975). *Milk and dairy foods.*

A detailed work for advanced study or for reference is by S. DAVIDSON (1972). *Human nutrition and dietetics* (Churchill-Livingstone).

Definitions and explanations of all terms likely to be met in reading about food and nutrition will be found in A. E. BENDER (1968). *Dictionary of nutrition and food technology* (Butterworths, London).

Index

Index

174   THE FACTS OF FOOD